SURVIVING JUDGEMENT DAY

Qaali Schmidt-Sorenson

CENTRAL PARK SOUTH PUBLISHING

Published by Central Park South Publishing 2023
www.centralparksouthpublishing.com

Typesetting and e-book formatting services by Victor Marcos

CONTENTS

FOREWORD

A Brief History of Somalia

The European colonial powers came to Somalia in 1869. In the 1880s, the area was divided into three parts: French Somaliland in the northwest (the country now called Djibouti), British Somaliland in the north and Italian Somaliland in the south.

The British colonization was resisted, and sheik Mohamed bin Abdullah Hassan organized a revolutionary Islamic movement that on four occasions triumphed over the colonial power in the period 1900-1904. It was not until 1920 that the British regained control of the area. In the late 1950s, the last years before Somalia's independence, Somalia's Ogaden region became part of Ethiopia, and Kenya took over the southern part of Somalia.

When the colonial powers left the country in 1960, North Somalia and South Somalia were combined to form what we call Somalia today. Somalia became an independent country, and the new constitution was one of Africa's most democratic and gave Somalis the right to form political parties. However, political life was unstable because of the many clan-based parties, and the first elected president, Osman Abd al-Rasheed Ali Shirmake, was assassinated in 1969.

General Siyaad Barre then took power in a military coup and was declared president on October 21, 1969. He remained in power until January 1991. He established a one-party regime with the Somalia Revolutionary Socialist Party as the only permitted party and banned people making public statements about which clan they belonged to.

In 1972, Somali replaced Italian, English and Arabic as the country's official language. The Somali language also became a written language. All Somalians were proud that Somali had become our official language.

In 1976, war broke out between Somalia and Ethiopia. The struggle was over the Ogaden region, and that war lasted until 1989. Ethiopia won. Many of our family members and acquaintances took part in the war, and many of them died.

INTRODUCTION

"Always Alone"

An essay on the dream of the desert
Who am I? What do I want? Who do I miss?

My soul slowly goes into decay because I've been separated so long from the desert. I can no longer bear to talk about that curse over my childhood—that terrible civil war I barely survived. I find it difficult to talk about war at all, or anything that is unpleasant and destroys human lives. I decided many years ago not to talk too much about death. Death is unpredictable and inevitable. It comes and goes, and we have little control over that. That has always been the case.

Instead, I would rather talk about the desert, about nature and the animals and people that live there. I often dream about the desert, the scent of it, and its soul and spirit. Over the past several years, I've had a great longing to revisit my family and homeland of Somalia. But most of my family has long since disappeared from there, and Somalia is all but invisible now, as if it no longer exists on the world map. I have always had a desire to return, to see the dear people and the beloved countryside before I die. Gradually, though, I am letting go of the idea of returning. How do you return to a place that no longer exists the way you remember it?

But if I were able, I'd most like to visit my father and reexperience a nomadic lifestyle. When I visited my father out in the bush, it was very different from my life in the city with my mother. The more I think about it now, the more fascinated I am of nomadic life. I was always proud of my father for sticking to the traditional nomadic lifestyle despite the hardships. I think back to my vacation stays with my father as a wonderful time where I wasn't controlled by other people, and where I had full freedom to do what I wanted and live according to my own desires. I miss many of the animals I interacted with there, especially giraffes, zebras, ostriches, and camels. When I visited him, he always slaughtered an animal such as a camel, and then there was feasting and dancing throughout the entire little nomadic village. Sometimes, when I was a teenager, I would dream I was living a different life, the life of a beautiful nomadic girl. Nomadic life seemed so strong and real to me—and still does.

The best thing about staying in the desert with my father was the rainy season. The desert was not barren and desolate, but full of life. During the rainy season, the desert was green and lush until the sun burned away the color again. There was so much to discover and learn in the desert. There are no traditional rules and duties. No prejudice. Neither hatred, revenge, nor condemnation. Nature is changeable and yet largely safe. Nomads live freely out there, a real life that many people only dream about. The question is, what is a real life for each individual human being?

One of my big dreams as a teenager was to meet a handsome and sweet young nomadic man and fall in love in the middle of the bush. We would fall in love at first sight, and our love would be so strong that soon after he would propose to me. After the courtship, he would promise that he would give everything he owned so he could marry me. I still remember how this fantasy played again and again in my head. Although I was a girl from a big city who went to high school like other Somalian city girls in the 1980s, I dreamed often about this ghost life—the life of a nomad girl.

Now, as I sit alone beside a blazing summer bonfire in Lolland, an island in Denmark, I think about the fires of the desert, and imagine I can see and hear a group of nomads dancing joyously around their own fire. When I look around at my view here in Lolland, I see beautiful open fields that are flat and green, with the sun disappearing from the sky in the distance. Despite the beauty of Lolland, I can't forget how much I miss the other life, the other land that is the Somalia desert.

In the desert, one cannot see where the horizon ends. The desert has its own history, its own charm and soul, which is immortal. Every night I see the desert in my mind, that lost land that was part of my childhood. Now it's part of my dream life, a distant and unreachable place I can only access through my imagination. The desert has always been a source of inspiration to me, an escape route to return to in my memories. Here in Lolland, I cannot smell the red earth or the scent of the acacia trees or the Indian Ocean with the blue salt water. But I can remember even the smallest things: the red sunsets, the great sandbanks, the lush green mountains, the thousand stars in the night sky. I hear the roar of lions and the sound of camels munching in the dark. The beauty of Lolland cannot erase these memories.

One afternoon not long ago, a cousin called and told me that my father was ill and might not have much longer to live. My father had asked my cousin to phone me. My cousin said I should hurry to Somalia if I wanted to see my father before he died. I have not seen my father since 1986. He was a nomad then and is a nomad still. When I spent time with my father, we did not celebrate birthdays. We didn't know what month or day it was, and we didn't care. We didn't think about age and appearance. Now, my experience has been that the more you think about appearance and age, the faster you grow old. You do not talk about age or how old you are or how old you will be on your next birthday. You simply live and let the years pass.

My father has led a good and long life. I have dreamed about seeing him once more before he dies, but unfortunately, I can't return to Somalia because there is still civil war and the Islamist terrorist group Al-shabab is active there. Since I'm married to a Dane and my last name is now Schmidt, my husband and I would be considered infidels and potential targets for terrorism and killing. I've been in exile in Europe for thirty years now, and as much as I long to return to my homeland, it's no longer possible. For the rest of my life, I will carry the pain and sorrow of not being able to return to that land of my childhood. I can only return to Somalia and my father in my dreams and memories, in the stories that I tell.

SURVIVING
JUDGMENT DAY

My First Childhood Years

When I was seven years old, I started first grade at a school in Mogadishu, Somalia. Even though I was a child, I knew that all Somalians were divided into clans. Yet at school, my classmates and I learned immediately that we were forbidden to say which clan we belonged to. There are three major clans in Somalia: the Darod, Isaaq, and Hawiye. In addition, there are three smaller ones: the Dir, Digil and Rahanweyn. All clans are divided into sub-clans. I belonged to the Marehan clan, a sub-clan of the Darod clan, but couldn't admit that to anyone.

In Somalia, girls are circumcised when they're still quite young. Most girls my age had already been circumcised by the time they started school. During recess, several girls would rush off to the bathroom to show each other their mutilated genitals. Sometimes they would vote on who had the nicest circumcision. Several of the girls had received the most extensive form of circumcision, which meant their vaginal openings had been stitched up and had only a tiny hole left for urine and menstrual blood to pass through. For these girls, peeing was both difficult and painful. Sometimes they had to sit on the toilet for half an hour to empty their bladders. Despite the pain of the circumcision, they were glad they had been circumcised. Now they were like all the other girls in Somalia.

I stayed away from the bathrooms as much as possible because I didn't want the other girls to know my shameful secret—that I hadn't been circumcised yet. If the other girls found out, I was afraid they would bully me. Whenever we went on a school outing to the ocean to learn how to swim, I kept on my underpants even though the other girls swam and bathed naked. The underpants irritated me—I wanted to throw myself naked and free into the waves like everyone else—but I was too afraid someone would notice I wasn't circumcised.

As I grew older, I became more curious and impatient about circumcision. One day I asked my cousin Sofie, who was twelve and circumcised, if I could see her genitals. We went behind the schoolyard and hid between a couple of houses. At first Sofie resisted my pleas and said she didn't want to show me anything. I begged some more, and eventually Sofie pulled down her clothes and exposed her genital area. I was amazed because I could not see anything but stitches and a small opening that was the entrance to her vagina. Everything else was gone. I squinted but didn't dare look closer. "Where are they?" I asked.

Sad and ashamed, Sofie pressed her legs together, pulled her underpants back into place, and stood up. "I don't want to talk about it anymore," she said.

I didn't want to embarrass Sofie further but also had a burning desire to know more. "How do you pee?" I asked.

Sofie looked away, and for a moment I thought she wasn't going to answer or would cry and run away. "The hole is for you to pee and menstruate and have babies," she said. She sounded like she was reciting information that had been told to her. "I don't like to talk about it."

The tone of her voice and the pain in her face began to scare me. "Did it hurt?" I asked in a whisper. "The circumcision?"

"Yes. I bled a lot." She turned back to face me and met my eyes. "Never get circumcised," she advised me.

One of my friends at school was named Maryan. She was a thin and coal black girl whose mother was a doctor at a city clinic as well as a history professor at the local university. Maryan, an only child, was a quiet girl but also stuffy and a little sad. Despite this, she was the smartest girl in the class. She read everything from children's books to women's magazines, whereas most of the rest of us didn't bother to read much. One day I asked Maryan if I could see her genitals. She didn't seem bothered by my request. We decided the school bathroom was too cold and clammy, so we went to a private place in the back of the schoolyard. "The whole thing was nasty," she said earnestly after we were finished. "You must refuse to get circumcised."

Her story resembled Sofie's. I was confused when I tried to picture the actual circumcision procedure. I couldn't understand why girls were circumcised if it caused so much pain and terror. But when I finally worked up the nerve and asked my mother what circumcision was like, she only said with a frown, "It hurts, but it's nothing you die from."

I wasn't sure if I believed her. My mother wasn't a kind or loving woman, and I didn't trust her. She'd grown up with nine brothers and had been neglected by her father, and this experience had toughened her and made her harsh, cold, and often distant. She was aggressive with all of us kids—my two older brothers, Rush and Wali, and sister Diina and me—and often yelled and struck us for no reason.

One day my mother pulled me aside and told me she'd arranged for my circumcision during summer vacation. We would travel to Baardheere about twelve hours away, where I would get circumcised along with three other girls on the same day. A "skilled" woman would perform the circumcision. My older sister Diina would join us, and we would turn the circumcision trip into a family vacation. My mother, divorced from my father, got time off work from her job as an office assistant at the Maritime Authority to make the trip. As time passed, I grew more uncertain about how to feel about my upcoming circumcision. On one hand, I was excited to get the circumcision so I could finally stop hiding my body and feel normal like everyone else. On the other hand, I was afraid of the procedure and the pain Sofie and Maryan had told me about. *Don't get circumcised:* their words echoed in my head like a warning.

When summer break arrived and the day came to travel to Baardheere, I felt uneasy and apprehensive. As the car rumbled down the road and Diina laughed and teased me, I was completely silent. I closed my eyes and pretended to sleep, but my mind was really in turmoil. We stopped for lunch at a nice restaurant, but I couldn't eat anything because I was too worried. My stomach was in knots.

My mother glanced over at me a few times and didn't bother to hide her irritation. "How are you feeling, Abdia?" she asked.

"I'm fine."

"You're not eating anything."

"I'm just tired," I said.

We spent the night in a grubby hotel in Baidoa, a border region between Somalia and Ethiopia. People in Baidoa, mostly nomads, dressed differently than most people in Somalia, usually wearing spotless white clothes and allowing their hair to grow Afro-style—thick and bushy. The hotel workers spoke a dialect we couldn't understand well, which only added to my feeling of discomfort. When my mother, Diina, and I drove down a Baidoa street, several people glared at us and even snapped pictures. I was glad when we left Baidoa the next morning.

Finally, we arrived in Baardheere. It was the season of the rains, which had turned everything—bushes, shrubs, fruit trees—green and lush. My mother warned me and Diina not to swim in the river because there were a lot of crocodiles around and many people had been pulled underwater and eaten, especially children. Since no one lived in my grandfather's house, that was where we would stay during our time in Baardheere. It was also where my circumcision would take place.

The next day we drove out to a small nearby village, surrounded by large fields where people were hunched over, working. I saw a bunch of elephants under a big tree, and nearby were zebras and large vultures perched on branches. "Who are we going to visit?" I asked my mother.

She told me that the lady who was going to circumcise me lived here, and that she needed to talk to her.

"Why do girls have to get circumcised?" I dared to ask my mother.

I saw how she stiffened whenever I brought up circumcision, and how her face turned cold and scolding. "Because that is our tradition and culture," my mother said.

"But why?"

"Don't ask questions." Her expression made it clear that she didn't feel like listening to me. I stopped talking because I didn't want her to hit me.

When we had been in Baardheere for a week, the lady who was going to circumcise me showed up at my grandfather's house. She was an older woman who resembled a scary witch. She was blind in one eye; I could see that it was completely white. She looked eerie, her hair long, tangled, and grey, and her face was covered with sharply marked wrinkles. She was wearing a long dirty black dress and smelled of sourdough. She didn't smile once the whole time. She terrified me.

I hurried over to my mother, who was laying out a clean tablecloth on the dining room table. "I don't want to be circumcised after all, Mama," I said. "I've changed my mind."

"Stop that!" she scolded me, smoothing out the wrinkles in the tablecloth. "You're a strong girl. Don't say such a thing."

Eventually, the other three girls came to the house with their mothers and other female family members. One by one they went into the dining room. Each circumcision took at least two hours, and each time the girl screamed and sobbed, her voice raw, harsh, frightened. I was standing outside with my mother but could still hear the screams. The searing sun beat down on my head, but I was too scared to feel the heat. My thoughts were jumbled and chaotic. Twice I pulled away from my mother and tried running back to the village where Diina was staying with a family member, but someone caught me both times and held me back. Finally, my mother grabbed my hand in a tight, pinching grip and refused to let go. We sat under a tree which provided what little shade there was and waited our turn for the circumcision. I tried to block out the sounds of the girls screaming, but I couldn't. Each cry was so painful I felt like I was the one getting cut into. A few times I screamed along with the circumcised girl, my cry melding with hers, a collective howl of pain. I begged my mother to put an end to this; it still wasn't too late for us to leave. But my mother ignored my pleas and my screams. She stared off in the distance and paid little attention to me. She just wanted the whole thing over with.

When it was my turn and I stepped into the dining room, I saw blood on the floor and splattered across the tablecloth. The woman with the white eye was sitting in a chair and had blood smeared across her hands, as did the two other women in the room, women who were paid to assist the witch lady and to hold me down during the circumcision. I stared into the faces of these women, but they didn't look back. They were as cold and distant as my mother. Part of me wanted to turn and run out of the house, but I knew my mother would catch me before I could get away, and there was no one around to help me. I was surrounded by women, including my mother, but was all alone.

Timidly and obediently, I lay on the dining room table while the women helped the witch lady to her feet and guided her over to the table. Then the other women held my legs while my mother pinned down my arms. I was not sedated. The witch lady with the white eye stood ready with a razor blade in her hand.

I could hear the blade cutting into my flesh. I screamed and tried to pull away, but my mother and the other women were holding me down too tightly. "Mama, please!" I sobbed. "Make her stop!"

But my mother did nothing. Her eyes were glazed as she tightened her hold on my thrashing arms. The witch woman continued to cut. At some point, the stress and pain were so unbearable that I went numb. The world seemed to dissolve around me. Nothing felt real.

When the witch woman was finished, she stitched me back up. Then my legs were tied together with strips of fabric from my hips and down to my ankles to prevent me from walking and possibly starting up the bleeding again. I had to lie with my legs together for four days and afterwards I had to be laced from the hip to the knees for another eight days. I'm not sure what happened to the other circumcised girls. I suppose they returned home with their mothers.

My mother and the other women placed me in a small room of my grandfather's house. I lay on a blanket on the floor under a tent. The witch lady with the white eye said I must sleep alone for the first four days. I must remain stationary in bed and not move. Exhausted from all the screaming and crying, I fell asleep at around noon. When it was seven o'clock in the evening, my mother brought me food. I started to cry. Why hadn't she helped me when I'd asked her to? Why was she never there for me when I needed her? She had betrayed me by listening to the witch woman instead of me.

I didn't eat or drink for a couple of days because I was so angry and hurt. Occasionally, my mother came into the dark room with a container for me to pee in, but I just shook my head defiantly and refused to do that too. I didn't urinate because I was afraid of the pain. During this time, I wasn't allowed to bathe. I only saw my mother when she stepped into the room to offer me food or tell me to brush my teeth. Otherwise, I lay on the floor all day and night, frightened and lonely, sometimes feeling weak and sick from the circumcision, without anyone to reassure me. Finally, I couldn't hold my water any longer. My mother held the container under me while I urinated in one long and painful gush.

After five days, the evil witch lady came again to check on me. I was bleeding more than was normal and my mother had grown worried. I was so furious at and scared of the witch lady that my body started shaking and I fainted. When I came to, I grabbed my mother's hand and shouted: "Mama, help me! Make her stay away!"

My mother tried to reassure me. "Abdia, she just needs to see how your genitals are doing," my mother said.

The witch lady stared down at me and was silent while I sobbed. I was just another faceless and terrified girl to her.

When I'd regained enough control, she spread out my legs and began her examination. She had a weird smile on her face as she poked and prodded. Her touch was rough, and I could tell she didn't care about me or any of the girls she operated on. Was it possible she took pleasure in cutting into girls and hearing their horrified screams? The witch lady told my mother there was inflammation in the wound because the stitching had "gone up" after I'd urinated too violently. She suggested that I get stitched up again after a few weeks, which would give my genitals time to heal. The witch woman recommended a treatment: my mother should dig a hole in the ground, fill it with leaves to burn, and then twice daily I should sit over the smoke rising from the hole. This method was supposed to help reduce inflammation. Then the witch lady walked off without another word to me or my mother.

My mother followed the witch lady's recommendation, but the smoke treatment did not help me. I felt the hot smoke rising between my legs and the sensitive area of my circumcision, and the burning sensation only made me feel more uncomfortable and afraid. I grew more and more sick. I couldn't eat anything now and felt tired and nauseous. My abdomen began to swell up.

After ten days I was hospitalized in Baardheere and given medicine to fight the infection. The doctor said I had to stay in the hospital until my pain was gone and I could urinate comfortably. I was hospitalized for a month. My family became upset and worried, and Diina was disappointed that her summer holiday had been ruined. My mother regretted choosing the old woman in the bush to circumcise me instead of taking me to a hospital in town. The witch woman who'd circumcised me had cut away too much and had cut it all wrong. Later, my mother admitted, she'd been afraid of losing me. I didn't remind her that she'd once told me circumcision was not something girls died from. After a few months, I was sewn together again at a private clinic once we'd returned to Mogadishu.

Circumcision has had a profound impact on my life because it's given me several problems over the years, including in my adult life. For example, I still experience a lot of pain when I'm menstruating. Plus, I had major problems when giving birth to my children. The doctors had to cut me open each time and deliver my babies through C-section. It took me a long time to recover from that. Despite my problems, I feel more fortunate than many Somali girls who have suffered even greater problems resulting from botched circumcisions. Some have died from infection or blood loss. Many have become sterile, and some have bad or painful sex lives as adults. And yes, some circumcised women have bled to death during childbirth.

While there has been a large decline in the number of Danish-Somalian girls who get circumcised, there are still some Danish-Somalian parents who, unable to move past the old Somalian ways, insist their daughters must get circumcised. Recently, when I attended a party at the Somalian Women's Association in Copenhagen, we discussed circumcision, and most women in attendance agreed that they wanted to help rid the world of this ancient and barbaric tradition. Unfortunately, there hasn't been a decrease in the number of girls getting circumcised in Somalia. There, circumcisions still take place in the same way they did when I was a child—in unsanitary conditions, with young girls getting operated on by an old bush woman with a blade.

The Teacher

At the Taleex School that I attended it was common for teachers to hit the students. One of my teachers, Adan Madowe, was especially harsh. He was a small, skinny, middle-aged man with short hair and very dark skin. He always seemed angry, which caused his eyes to bulge so large and white that the children were afraid to make eye contact with him. He chewed tree leaves called khat and was a heavy smoker. He smoked in the principal's office and the classrooms, and even smoked when conducting meetings with parents. Because of this, Mr. Madowe's clothes always smelled like ashes.

Whenever Mr. Madowe was having a bad day, he would take his aggression out on one of the students. During breaks he would often grab a stick from a tree and start chasing and shouting at any of the students who rubbed him the wrong way. If he caught a student, he beat the student with the stick all over his or her body. When the other teachers hit us, they only struck the palms of our hands. All the students were afraid of Mr. Madowe and avoided him as much as possible.

One day during recess, I started to not feel well. My face felt flushed, and my stomach hurt. I wondered if I should ask Mr. Madowe for permission to go home. I was reluctant to approach him, but finally gathered up my nerve and went inside to our classroom. The door was closed; Mr. Madowe always kept the door closed because he couldn't stand the sound of the children laughing and playing outside during recess. I knocked on the door and entered. He was sitting behind his desk, waiting for recess to end, smoking a cigarette and chewing on a khat leave. There was a book on his desk, but it wasn't open. Mr. Madowe tapped his hand on the desk and stared at me without compassion as I timidly approached his desk.

"Excuse me, Mudane Macalin," I said. In the Somali language, 'Mudane Macalin' means 'Mr. Teacher.' "I'm sick. Can I please go home?"

He glared at me, his eyes hard and feverish. "Why are you standing there?" he shouted at me. He took the cane from behind his desk, grabbed my arm and started beating me. He struck my head, shoulders, back, legs. While he beat me, he continued to shout so fast and loud he was soon out of breath. "Troublesome, unruly kid!" he grunted, all the while still chewing on the khat hanging from a corner of his mouth. Terrified, I tried to pull away, but his grip was too strong, and he was standing in front of the door so I couldn't escape. I started to cry and shouted for help. A couple of teachers out in the hall peered inside, but they only shook their heads and laughed at my beating. Finally, I pulled away long enough to run out of the classroom. I ran down the hall, out of the building, across the schoolyard and outside the school gate. I threw myself down on the cool ground and sobbed uncontrollably. The beating had caused my stomach to ache more, to the point where I felt I might vomit.

Soon an elderly woman walked up to me, a large, fat woman with a kind face and peaceful soul. She was wearing a colorful, soothing dress that reminded me of a butterfly. "What's wrong, my little girl?" she asked me. "Do you have bad skin?"

She must have asked this strange question because she noticed my red and swollen face from where Mr. Madowe had struck me. I sobbed even harder as I told her the story of my beating.

After I'd finished talking, the old woman shook her head and patted my arm. "I would very much like to ask your teacher why he beats the children," she said, her voice trembling with anger. "Who gave him permission to beat other people's children?" She put her arm around my shoulders and pulled me close to her, and in her arms, I felt some hope return. "Everything will be fine," she said. "Don't worry. You should not have to see that teacher ever again. He should never work at this school again. I'll take care of that."

She led me over to a nearby cart that sold food and bought me a large mango popsicle. She told me her name was Haawo and she lived next to the school. As it turned out, her two children had also attended this school and had also been beaten by teachers.

Haawo and I returned to the school and went directly to the principal's office. "We would like to speak to the principal," she told the woman working in the office.

The woman looked nervous when she asked Haawo why she wanted to speak to the principal. After Haawo told her, the woman pointed to a chair in a corner of the school office and asked me to sit down. Then she went behind the desk and entered a room that was the principal's office. She left the door ajar, so Haawo and I heard her speaking loudly and angrily to the principal about our complaint.

After a pause, the principal stepped out of his office and approached us. He was a tall and suave man, always dressed well, who was quiet and calm but also disinterested in what was happening to the children inside the school. Whether he was depressed or just not interested in his work, I never knew. "How can I help you?" he asked, eying us both indifferently.

Before Haawo could start talking, he shook his head, held up his hand, and returned to his office. Through the open door I could see him open a small refrigerator next to his desk, remove a can of Coca-Cola, and open it before he returned to Haawo and I with the soda in his hand. He took a long sip, then sat down nearby and asked us again what he could do for us.

"Well, it's been a long time, hasn't it?" Haawo said to the principal. She returned his stare and did not waver.

"Yes," he answered, taking another sip from his Coca-Cola.

"You have not changed, but today something must be done to change this school. One of your teachers has beaten this poor child. Your other teachers are doing the same thing to their students. Why is this, Mr. Husein?"

Haawo was clearly angry, her body shaking in fury. And yet the principal only smiled back at us, unbothered. "Well, students have to be disciplined," he told Haawo. He spoke like a man who was accustomed to always being in control and didn't care to have his authority questioned.

"There are many parents who are dissatisfied with this school," Haawo continued as if the principal hadn't spoken. "I wonder what would happen if all of us parents got together and went to the municipal authorities to complain about this school?"

Instantly, the principal's uninterested look faded and was replaced by concern. He looked like a little mouse caught by a cat. "I'm sure it won't be necessary to take up this incident with parents and the school board," he said uncertainly.

"We'll see about that," Haawo said as she grabbed my hand and led me out of the office. She slammed the door on our way out. I smiled, thrilled by the slam and proud of the way Haawo had stood up to the principal. "I would like to meet with your mother on Thursday," Haawo told me. "You had better stay home from school until then."

I thanked her and we shook hands before leaving.

When I got home, my mother was talking to the neighbor's wife outside our house. I started to cry again. My mother and the neighbor hurried over. "What is wrong with you?" my mother asked, horrified.

I held out my hands and arms so she could see the red marks from the teacher's beating. I showed her the bruises on my shoulders. I started to tell what had happened, but I was sobbing so hard that the words became garbled.

My mother rushed into the house and returned a moment later with her handbag slung over her shoulder. "Come on now," she said. "You show me that teacher who did this to you."

"I don't want to see him again!" I couldn't help but think how my mother often hit me and my siblings, but when someone else hit us, she was angry and defensive. I told my mother about Haawo and how she had intervened and wanted to speak to her. "Please, Mama," I said again. "I don't want to see the teacher anymore today."

It was difficult for my mother to wait until tomorrow to speak to Mr. Madowe, but she understood that it was too late now to meet with the teachers. Eventually, my mother spoke with Haawo, and together they decided that all the parents should go to the city authorities and tell them about what was happening at the Talaax School and how dissatisfied they were by how their children were treated. The mayor listened to the parents' concerns and promised the school would improve. The principal was promptly fired, but Mr. Madowe was not fired, nor were all the teachers who had watched my beating and laughed. I became depressed and lost interest in going to school because I was afraid of additional punishment. I asked my mother if I could stay home for a while and not attend school. She allowed me to do this, but after two weeks, I started missing school terribly. Since I wanted to return to school but didn't want to face any of the teachers at the Talaax School, I asked my mother about getting moved to a different school.

Arrangements were made, and soon I started at a new elementary school called Hodan. It was further away from my house but also had higher ethical standards for the teachers. The neighbor's daughter, Sarah, attended this school, and I was driven daily to the new school along with Sara by Sara's family's driver. I enjoyed being with Sarah. I learned quickly that Sara was quiet and reserved, who liked staying at home and didn't play around much with other kids. But she was also kind and tranquil. In her presence, I felt myself growing kinder and more relaxed. I thought I could trust her, and as we became friends, she grew loyal and never demanded anything from me.

My First War

I was eleven when I experienced my first war. I was too young then to understand anything about the mounting tensions between Somalia and Ethiopia. During summer vacation from school, I went to visit my Aunt Halimo in Garbaharey. She had no children herself, so my brothers, Diina and I were like her surrogate children, and she loved and pampered us as if we were her own. She lived in a small, white-brick house located in the center of town. Outside she had a spacious palm terrace with garden furniture, where she liked to sit with her friends and drink tea. Sometimes she slept out on the terrace because it was too hot inside the house. Nearby was a well-kept garden, where she grew watermelon, corn, and mango.

I soon became friends with the neighbor's daughter, Hani. Hani was my age, a tall and happy girl who laughed a lot and was wildly funny. She was different from my friends at home. Often, there was competition between my girlfriends back in Mogadishu. We quarrelled a lot and gossiped behind each other's backs. Hani was not like that. Because she was growing up in what appeared a happy and well-adjusted family that didn't place restrictions on her, she was relaxed and free-spirited and never felt the need to compete with me.

On a morning when it was too hot to play outside, I sat in one of the rooms of my aunt's house with Hani. We were building small houses for our homemade wooden dolls. The dolls were made with sticks of caday wood that Hani and I had tied together. We made the dolls' hair by first beating the thinnest twigs of the wood against the floor and then chewing the twigs until they became soft.

While Hani and I were playing, three of my aunt's girlfriends stopped by to visit. Unexpected guests often dropped by to visit my aunt. My aunt greeted her friends and they sat in the living room instead of the terrace garden to drink coffee, eat cake, talk, and laugh. They all wore clean and brightly-colored dresses. Hani and I turned our attention back to the dolls.

Suddenly we heard the distant roaring of airplanes. Hani and I glanced up from our dolls and then looked at each other, confused. Garbaharey had a small runway which was only used in emergencies, such as if someone was in urgent need of hospitalization, or if a governmental official was visiting the region. The sound of a plane was not something we were used to. Hani and I ran into the living room. One of my aunt's friends hurried outside still holding her cup of coffee, and she spilled some of the coffee over her dress but didn't notice as she peered up into the sky. Another woman clutched a napkin with some cake inside. The third woman was calmer, and she rose from her chair more slowly, pausing to slice another section of cake before she followed us outside, leaning on her cane. My aunt and her friends exclaimed and wondered aloud what was happening, and then they went silent, speechless.

Many other people from up and down the street also rushed outside to see what all the commotion was about.

Five fighter jets were approaching, flying low and then shooting with lightning speed back up in the air. The sounds were loud and deafening. "What is that sound?" one of my aunt's friends cried out and dropped her coffee cup onto the ground. Another of my aunt's friends, who lived down the street from us, started shouting for her children, who were at school. My aunt was also flustered by the planes and called me to her side. The adults were more frightened than Hani and I were.

Hani and I soon lost interest in the planes and went back inside to resume playing with our dolls. We sat back down and had just picked up our toys when there was the sound of an explosion nearby, so loud and fierce the house shook. I could feel the vibrations in the ground, like we were in the middle of an earthquake. Hani and I were young, but we knew those explosions were from bombs dropped on the city. Hani and I threw our dolls on the floor and ran back screaming to the adults, who were hurrying in from outside, covering their heads and crying in alarm.

"What's happening?" I cried to my aunt.

"I do not know, my girl," she said. "Come here to me."

One of my aunt's friends shouted that we should take cover, so I dashed off alone to my aunt's bedroom and hid under the bed. But no one else had followed me to her room, and soon I grew scared of being alone, so I ran into a different room where everyone else had gone. It was clear Aunt Halimo and her girlfriends knew nothing about why we were getting bombed. Another explosion followed, even louder this time. I crawled under the bed where Hani was. We held our hands to our ears but that did little to block out the deafening noise. Hani's mother had come over from next door, and she hurried over and squeezed under the bed next to us and squeezed Hani's hand. Aunt Halimo and the other women crouched on the floor and began praying. The calmer friend of my aunt told us all not to worry and that everything would be okay.

But I was worried—worried and scared. I believed strongly in Allah and had been told he could save us if we prayed to him. I was afraid to die because I didn't know if I was good enough to get into Heaven. Even though I had fasted during Ramadan and prayed to Allah before, what if that wasn't enough? When Judgment Day came, people would get divided into two groups: the righteous would go to heaven and the sinful to hell. I didn't want to spend eternity with the sinners, so I pressed my hands together and let the words flow:

Allah, help me. You are great.
I ask you for help today.
I don't know what I shall do.
I am not strong enough.
Allah, I believe in you. I am a pious child. I ask you
for help today.
Allah, what is that sound? Oh, Allah, we are good
people who believe in you. I ask you for help today.
Allah, I want to see my family again. I ask you for
help today.
Allah, I do not want to die now because I am only
11 years old. Please help me. I ask you for help today.

Finally, after another half an hour of explosions, the bombing stopped. The roar of the planes subsided. I crawled tentatively out from under the bed, wiped the dust from my hands, and thanked Allah for answering my prayer. We all looked at each other, stunned and confused, unsure what to do next. "It is God's will this happened," one of my aunt's friends said, her voice shaking. "This is punishment from God."

Then the city sirens started to wail. We hurried back into the living room to look out the windows. A couple of the women cracked the door open to listen outside. "Don't open the doors!" someone cried, I wasn't even sure who. "Don't let anyone see you. We have to keep hiding!"

Slowly, it was dawning on us that all the explosions and bombing was not God's will, but that we were at war. We weren't sure if only planes had been sent to bomb us, or if enemy soldiers had also marched into the city and were now out in the streets. We all stood around, looking at each other, confused and frightened.

I went to my aunt and took her hand. "I'm ready to go home now," I said, my voice small and tentative.

"Calm down, my girl," she said and squeezed my hand back. Her hand was shaking and sweaty. "We will find a way to get you home."

I didn't say anything more. I moved to the window and glanced out along with a couple of the other women. Dust and smoke like from a tornado hung over the streets. Occasionally, we heard a human scream or wail coming from somewhere. I thought, maybe, that a neighbor's house had been hit. Everything felt surreal, like a bad dream. Garbaharey was a small town and peaceful; it didn't seem possible it could have been thrown into such chaos so quickly.

Then we heard sirens going off. Soon military trucks, tanks, and jeeps were driving down the streets. Men in uniform were speaking through megaphones, telling us there was war in the city and we had to remain indoors until they knew it was safe to come outside. In the distance, we heard gunshots and artillery fire, which turned out to be Somalian soldiers in the surrounding mountains shooting at the Ethiopian planes.

Everyone obeyed the soldiers' orders and stayed inside. We didn't dare step outside in all the dust and noise and ruined houses. Then the soldiers and their vehicles passed by again, telling us through megaphones that we should all leave the city temporarily until the fighting and bombing had ceased. "There's going to be more bombings?" one of my aunt's friends asked.

We all stayed inside and waited. When sunset arrived, we cautiously went outside to survey the damage. I was horrified at the sight of bombed houses and buildings, and the burning chemical smell hanging in the air. Several corpses were lying out on the street near the main road. One of my mother's friends whispered a prayer, then my aunt and some of her friends, as well as other people in the neighborhood, did what they could to help. We covered the dead bodies with blankets and clothes. My aunt and her friends started going down the street and knocking on the doors of all the houses to see who was alive and who wasn't. I stayed hidden for much of this search because I couldn't bear the sight of dead bodies and pets. I was afraid I would be sick. The dead bodies had to be buried when it was dark, we were told, and the military would help.

Now that it was almost dark and people were outside, my aunt and some other people approached the military soldiers who were out in the streets. We learned that the Ethiopians had chosen to attack Garbaharey because Siyaad Barre, the president of Somalia, and his clan lived here. We were also told that more troops and weapons were headed to the city as a safety precaution. The soldiers didn't expect that additional attacks would occur, but they were prepared if that happened. By having people leave the city and hide outside of town, they could ensure that people wouldn't gather in the streets and become targets if the bombers came again. They advised us to pack our things and hide out in the mountains or in the bush areas outside of town where the planes could not see us. We should travel in small groups and make sure not to spend time near large animals such as cows and camels, because fighter jets flew low and could easily spot large animals. Even the color of our clothes was important. The soldiers told us to avoid white, red, or blue clothes. If we were going to use tents, make sure they were green or sand-colored because these were not as easily spotted from the sky. They advised us to stay in holes or caves in the mountains if we could because those were safest. When we had to make a fire to cook food, we should do it inside a cave or else bombers would see the smoke from the sky. While we were speaking to the soldiers, I hid behind my aunt and clutched her hand. I was afraid to let go because I was afraid of being alone.

For several days, my aunt and I, and everyone in Garbaharey, were afraid to leave our houses. The friend of a friend, Geed Guled, a 70-year-old man who had survived World War II and served as a Somalian freedom fighter in the struggle against the colonial powers, came to our house to give us advice about what we should do during wartime. For one, he advised us to leave our home only after sunset. The darkness gave us cover and made us less visible to any potential bombers.

"Is it doomsday yet?" I couldn't help but ask him.

He smiled but his smile looked weary. "It's not doomsday," he told me. "This has nothing to do with religion. It's politics. Those were Ethiopian planes that bombed us."

At that time, there was a military base located in the mountains surrounding Garbaharey. Since no one had expected Ethiopian planes to bomb us, most of the Somali soldiers were sleeping or shopping in the city when the bombing occurred. A lot of people were killed, mostly children from the Koran school which was open during the summer holidays. When the children heard the planes, they grew excited and ran outside to see what all the commotion was about. The teachers tried to keep them inside the classrooms, but the children ignored them. The Koran school was located on the outskirts of the city, a large building clearly visible from the air and an easy target for the bombers. The children in their white school uniforms also made easy targets. The others killed were mostly traders in the bazaar who couldn't find shelter, and people in houses that were randomly struck by the bombs.

The bombing and the thought of more bombings terrified me. My aunt tried to reassure me, but it didn't help much because I could see that she was also scared and confused. No one knew what would happen next or how safe the streets were. During the day everyone stayed inside, and the streets were eerily quiet and deserted. At night, under the cloak of darkness, people started to move around outside like stealthy nocturnal animals, careful and on our guard. My aunt and I shopped at night along with everyone else, and we walked down the dark aisles of the store lighted by only a few well-placed candles. We bought rice, corn, pasta, oil, tea, sugar, dates, cupcakes, and Oodkac, which was dried beef that could last for several months in a cupboard. We had to squint to see in the dim and flickering light.

Because the soldiers had told us to leave the city as soon as possible, many residents agreed to hide in a cave far up in the mountains. My aunt woke me up at 4 a.m. one morning so we could make the climb to the mountains. Many people made these trips, groups coming from several directions in the city. The rule was that people should travel in small groups of no more than ten people for reduced visibility, which would make everyone safer. Getting up so early and walking for hours was difficult, especially when we had to carry our food, drinks, and blankets because Aunt Halimo didn't own a car. Some people did have cars but thought it was better to walk than to drive because a car could be spotted more easily from the air. We walked down a long and winding road that twisted up into the mountains. I was sleepy and couldn't see because it was still dark. I tripped and fell on the road, crushing some eggs that we had brought along from my aunt's chickens. I was too tired to care, and just picked myself up and continued walking with everyone else.

The trip took four to five hours to complete. We couldn't walk fast because we had so much to carry and were traveling with older people and small children. Finally, we reached a large cave in the mountains which had previously been home to a lion. The cave still smelled like a predator. We set down our food, drinks, and blankets and slumped to the ground, exhausted. We looked like a big family out on a picnic, but we were scared, tired, and displaced, afraid of what the future might bring.

Still, since we had to spend our days and nights in this cave, we tried to make the situation as pleasant as possible. We ate our food, drank tea, and chatted with one another. Some of the young men had brought their guns along and went out hunting for deer. Once, one of the men got lucky and killed a doe. He brought the carcass back to the cave and we grilled the meat over a big fire we started from dry branches, twigs, and pieces of shrubs. Some of the elders told us they didn't think it was a good idea to make a bonfire since planes might easily spot the smoke and flames from the air, so after that we started boiling the meat along with our rice and pasta. By the second week we grew calmer and less scared of detection, and we started to grill after sunset. We hung out clothes near the fire and stood outside to talk and relax.

Despite the uncertain circumstances, I liked staying on the mountain. Once I grew less afraid of the situation, I sometimes went exploring away from our camp. There were beautiful red and grey stones I'd never seen before, and some of the trees were exotic and different than what I was used to seeing in Garbaharey. The birds were also of different colors and sizes. Once I went out hunting for quadrupeds and chameleon lizards. I liked the countryside, the breeze, the stillness. In the distance, I could see Garbaharey, and it looked sad, abandoned, and dead.

After two weeks in the cave, Aunt Halimo decided we needed to make a return trip to Garbaaharrey. "We need to pick up more food and drink," she said. "And I want to take a bath."

Although Aunt Halimo didn't have a car, her neighbor did. One day he suggested we drive with him to a different mountain the next day, about six miles from town. His car wasn't that big, but we still camouflaged it with large branches and multiple leaves. About two miles from the cave Aunt Halimo and I were going to, our neighbor dropped us off and drove on to another place. As we were walking the rest of the way to the cave, we ran across a nomad family who were tending to their camels, cows, and goats. The family, a married couple with three children, lived on the mountain in some makeshift huts. From an airplane one would not be able to see the huts, which were made of grass and wood and blended in with the natural surroundings. The family invited us to dinner inside one of the huts, which we gratefully accepted.

The family slaughtered a lamb, roasted the meat over an open fire, and served us fresh corn to go along with the meat. We were given several choices of milk: cow's milk, goat's milk, camel's milk. They also had a large selection of milk products such as raw milk, buttermilk, and cream cheese. One drink was made of tea, milk, and sugar boiled together, and it tasted good although it was as sweet as candy. Before we ate, we washed our hands and sat on the ground. We were somewhat embarrassed about eating and drinking so much food from this family who had so little. While we ate, the nomad family told us how afraid they were of planes spotting their animals. The bombings made it impossible for the animals to roam free because they were scared and skittish of the noise.

Mostly, though, the family was quiet and watched us eat. They seemed happy we were enjoying their food so much. At one point the children noticed a frog near the doorway, and they started playing with the frog and named it Tok. Several beautiful butterflies of different colors fluttered into the house, some of them alighting on us. I tried to catch one, but Aunt Halimo scolded me. "Stop, my girl," she said. "We are guests."

"Okay," I said, embarrassed that I'd embarrassed my aunt. Since we were guests, we were supposed to behave properly.

Occasionally, flies would land in someone's milk. This made me squeamish, but the nomad family calmly picked the flies from out of their glasses and drank the milk. There were also several spiders, red and black and yellow, crawling around the hut. The spider webs on the ceiling were beautiful, but I was still scared of the spiders.

By the end of the meal, my stomach was bloated and looked like a frog's belly. I felt a bit sick. When we were leaving, my aunt offered the family some money, but they would not accept it. They were accustomed to selling their milk in town, they told us, but now that there were so few people around, they couldn't sell anything. Since they couldn't drink all the milk themselves, it was better for us to drink some of the milk than for them to have to throw the milk out.

We thanked them many times for their hospitality and agreed that we would come the next day to buy milk and meat from them. We did as we promised and brought sugar and sweets for them as gifts. Aunt Halimo, who ran a small women's clothing store on the main street in town, brought some women's and children's clothes for them to keep. The nomad family was happy to receive our gifts, and the children were delighted with the sweets since they had never tasted them before.

Eventually, people grew tired of moving back and forth between the city and the mountains, and we decided to return to the city and stay there. But it was boring to remain inside all the time. People were still afraid that the Ethiopian planes would return. Aunt Halimo let me leave the house and play with Hani next door, and sometimes my aunt's friends came over for tea, just as they had before the war started.

One day I received a letter from my family in Mogadishu. They'd heard about the bombing attack and wrote to say how much they missed me. My mother told me I should come home soon and remove myself from the danger in Garbaharey. I cried after I read the letter and was reminded how much I missed my family, my mother's scolding and my brothers' teasing.

I sat down with my aunt in the living room, still holding the letter in my hand. "My mother wants me to go back to Mogadishu," I said. "Will you come with me?"

I was afraid to travel alone under the circumstances but also didn't want my aunt stuck in Garbaharey by herself. "I can't, Abdia," she said. "I will come visit another time, though." When she saw the disappointment on my face, she added, "Who would look after the house if I'm away? I have the shop and my animals."

The shop was closed after the bombing, so I didn't understand why Mina couldn't check in at the store from time to time if Aunt Halimo came with me to Mogadishu. Mina was a young woman in her twenties who did a lot of the work in the store. Before the bombing started, when I was bored and restless, sometimes I would go and visit Mina. She would give me a cup of tea or a bottle of Fanta, and we would chat together.

My aunt didn't personally take care of the animals she owned—cows, sheep, goats. They were cared for by a nomadic family who lived in the desert, so why couldn't the nomad family continue to take care of the animals and my aunt could come to Garbaharey with me? Soon, though,

I came to understand that my aunt lived a balanced and harmonious life here in Garbaharey and had many friends, and she didn't want to leave it all behind. At least if she remained in town, she could take frequent trips to the store and make sure there were no break-ins.

"I don't want you to be alone," I said and thought of her ducking under the kitchen table during another bombing.

"Don't worry about me," Aunt Halimo said and patted my hand. "I'll be fine. And we'll find someone who can take of you on the ride back to Mogadishu."

"Okay." I could tell she was being strong for my sake. An idea occurred to me. "I'll stay one more week," I told her.

My aunt smiled, and I saw how pleased she was that she'd have my company for a while longer.

A couple days later, refugees from Ethiopia, mostly people who were originally from Somalia, began arriving in Garbaharey and Baardheere because they were close to the Ethiopian border. They came from cities where there were wars and political unrest. If they'd stayed in their own country, they might have been considered traitors and shot by the Ethiopian army. This was the first time I'd heard the word refugee. They looked and smelled different than what I was used to in the city. They wore mostly white clothes with blue stripes, and their hair was often swept to one side and very thick. The refugees would eat pretty much anything, including sheep's head, which I found strange. At night they made bonfires and sat next to each other and sang, but I couldn't understand what they were saying. They were quite poor and couldn't afford food and a place to live.

A group of about thirty refugees settled under the trees near my grandfather's house. My grandfather had died before

I was born, and members of my family had inherited his house and property. The refugees had nothing with them, not even food and a change of clothes. They didn't say much, and I could tell that these people were from the countryside. When I looked into their eyes, they just gazed back calmly. When people were able to, they offered the refugees leftover food and used clothes. I thought it was a shame for the refugees to have to live under the trees, because it was often windy and sometimes rained. I asked my aunt if we could give them clothes and blankets, but she said we didn't have enough to help so many people. However, she did offer a few items of clothing to some of the older people who had nothing. One time I gave some of the children my own clothes—a couple of purple and yellow dresses, a blouse, and a pair of old shoes. I handed the clothes to a girl who I thought would fit into my clothes. The girl and her mother thanked me while staring down at the ground. Afterwards, Aunt Halibo scolded me. "You need your clothes for yourself," she said.

One day, my aunt asked if I would go with her to visit her friend, Ayan, who lived on a farm about twelve miles from Garbaharey. I agreed since living in the city had grown boring—we were still staying inside all day in case there was another bombing attack. Maybe if I were out in the countryside, I could experience something new and have more freedom. The next day my aunt and I went to a store and bought tea, salt, dates, a few kilos of sugar and a liter of gas. These were items that people in the countryside needed when they didn't have the opportunity to shop in the city very often. My aunt didn't have a car and neither did her girlfriend, so we would have to walk the twelve miles out to the farm. I wasn't sure how we would carry all the items we'd bought for that long distance. My aunt decided I should carry the dates, the gas bottle, and the tea packages, and she would carry the heaviest items—the sugar, salt, and two liters of water.

We left early the next morning. Garbaharey is the hottest city in southern Somalia because it lies in the middle of four mountains, and although it rains occasionally, the area is mostly dry. The best time to walk was between five and eleven o'clock, before the sun became unbearably hot. We went out to the main road, but even there, traffic was light. You could walk a long way without passing any cars, especially so early in the morning. When we'd walked about three miles, I grew tired, so we sat down at the roadside to rest. My shoulders felt tight, and my arms ached from all the carrying. My feet were hot and sore. My aunt started telling me stories to make me forget how tired I was. She told me a lot about her life when she was young, including about the men she had fallen in love with. I thought her stories were exciting; my mother never shared this kind of intimate detail about her own life.

But no matter how many stories my aunt told to try to distract me, and no matter how much she encouraged me, I couldn't walk anymore. My legs and feet simply felt too weak. The sun began to rise and soon the day would grow hotter. As we sat thinking about what to do, two young men walked toward us. They were walking fast and looking directly at us. Scared, I grabbed my aunt's hand. Maybe the men would decide to rape us. Hani had told me a story once about a group of men who had raped a woman. I pinched Aunt Halimo's arm in warning, but she only gave me a piercing glance. "Calm down!" she said.

The men stopped and greeted us. They were well dressed in clean clothes, but they were nomad clothes with a lot of bright colors. Their hair was big and bushy, but they had no beards. When they smiled, they looked friendly and pleasant, and my fear of them died away. They were brothers, one tall and one short. Because my aunt had been born and raised in this area, she asked the young men who their fathers were, thinking she might know them. The shorter man talked for both himself and his brother, and he started talking about families they knew, where they were going, and where we were going. "We can help you carry your stuff," the shorter man said. "We're going in the same direction."

My aunt thanked them, and the two men picked up our stuff and walked along with us. As it turned out, the young men didn't find our things very heavy. The time passed more quickly as we walked along the deserted road and the day grew brighter. After we'd walked over six miles, I was convinced I could finish the rest of the trip. The company of the young men was invigorating, and I no longer felt as tired as I once had.

The men said they were spending the night with their parents in an area near Ayan's farm, so they knew the family we were visiting. "We have to walk all tomorrow too," the short man said. "We're going to a wedding. It's about fifty miles away."

Fifty miles? I couldn't imagine walking that far. I hadn't said a word since the two men started walking with us, but when they mentioned a wedding, I grew curious. I wanted to know the details of this wedding, but I was shy about talking to strangers, especially men, and didn't dare ask any questions.

Several times along the way, we took breaks and drank some water, or splashed water into our hands and wiped our faces and throats with it. Soon we'd reached Ayan's house. Ayan stepped out of the house and invited the young men inside for a cup of tea, but they politely said no, since they were supposed to meet up with friends. The young men looked happy and fresh as they walked away.

Ayan, a farmer's wife, had a 12-year-old daughter named Sofie and a 15-year-old boy named Ali. In the beginning, I had a hard time talking to Sofie and Ali because they seemed shy and embarrassed about their poverty. Also, they spoke in a thick dialect that was hard to understand. After a few hours, Sofie and I grew more comfortable with each other. She brought me out back to see their animals. There was a fat, lazy cow lying under a tree and barking while flicking its tail at the flies. The cow didn't like other cows or animals, and every time an animal came near it, the cow stood up long enough and charged with its horn before returning to its position under the tree. There was a male chicken that was filthy and pecked at everything, and a lonely donkey that snorted and cried frequently. Because I was from the city, Sofie was interested in hearing about Mogadishu, the school I attended, and why I was visiting my aunt for so long. She talked so much about nature and rural life that I completely forgot about my fear that the Ethiopian planes would return.

"I don't go to school," Sofie told me. "I have to work here on the farm." But she admitted that she'd like to attend school to meet other children and learn math, science, history, and reading.

I wasn't much interested in natural science classes at school, but now that I was with Sofie, I was curious about nature and wanted to learn more before I returned home to Mogadishu. For example, I didn't know anything about how to cultivate the land and harvest crops. Sofie explained it in a way that made it easy to understand. I thought it was difficult to cultivate a field and care for it, but according to Sofie, it really wasn't.

We walked to the family field where both corn and melons were growing. I noticed one especially large watermelon and pointed it out. "Look!" I exclaimed. "How can a watermelon grow so big? You'd need two men to carry it."

Sofie shrugged. "We have a lot of big melons," she said proudly. "Do you want to eat one of them?"

"Yes," I said, laughing. "But won't your parents get mad?"

"No. Ali and I are allowed to eat anything we want."

We sat down next to a melon patch under some of the largest corn stalks for shade, and we ate a couple of the watermelons. I ate more than Sofie because I was thirsty after the long walk to the farm, and the ripe watermelons cooled my throat.

My aunt and I stayed with Ayan and her family for three days. Since my aunt and Ayan had known each other since they were small, we felt comfortable staying on the farm, especially since Ayan's husband was traveling in northern Somalia and so was not around. We learned a lot about Ayan and her husband's future plans. Because they raised cows, sheep, and chickens and grew corn, watermelons, and tomatoes, they spent virtually no money on food. Still, they wanted to grow onions and other vegetables that they couldn't grow here because the soil was too dry. Eventually, they wanted to move closer to the Jubba River because the soil was richer there and more suitable for growing, and conditions would be better for their animals as well.

When Aunt Halimo and I prepared to leave the farm, Sofie looked sad, so I promised we would see each other again the next time I was on vacation visiting my aunt. Now that my aunt and I had walked the entire distance from Garbaharey to the farm, I was convinced I could walk all the way back without problems since we had nothing to carry. But we'd only walked a few miles when a large truck came along. The driver stopped and offered us a ride. It's a custom in Somalia for drivers to stop and ask pedestrians if they need a ride, since very few people can afford to own a car or pay for transport. My aunt and I climbed in the back of the truck, and although the road was terribly bumpy and the driver drove slowly, which emphasized the bumps, my aunt and I were pleased we'd get home earlier than expected.

When we arrived back in Garbaharey, there were still not many people around, and only a few shops were open. My aunt decided to go out and see what the city's situation was like. "You stay here," my aunt said. "There's no reason for both of us to be outside if the planes come again."

At the mention of the planes, all my fears of another bombing attack came swooping down around me. "I want to come with you," I said.

"Abdia—"

"I don't want to be alone if the planes come," I pleaded, and eventually my aunt relented and said I could come with her.

We didn't venture out far, just to our neighbor's place. They were happy to see us and invited us inside for tea and cookies. We learned that the situation around the city was pretty much the same as it had been since the bombing attack. Everything was uncertain, no one felt secure, and many families had moved out into the countryside where they felt safer. The people who remained in the city still stayed inside for most of the day and only went outside for walks or to visit family or friends in the evening, when darkness shielded them.

When my aunt and I returned home, we sat quietly on the sofa. My fear of the planes and the bombing, which I'd been able to forget when out at Ayan and her husband's farm, now grew stronger and more immediate. "Will you teach me to pray to Allah five times a day?" I asked my aunt.

She turned to me with a quizzical expression. "Isn't that what we're supposed to do?" I added. "Pray five time a day."

"Yes, that's right. I'd be happy to show you." She smiled. "I'm proud that you're asking me about that."

Aunt Halimo was very diligent in showing me the correct way to pray. First, we washed our hands, face, and feet so we were clean before God. Then we went to a rug spread in the center of the floor and kneeled. Aunt Halimo read something in Arabic from a book, then we bowed up and down four times. When we started to pray, I followed my aunt's examples and mimicked her words.

At the end of the week, as we'd planned, I returned to Mogadishu. I couldn't stand the tension and uncertainty of Garbaharey anymore. My mother and brothers and sister all cried when they saw me. It felt good to be home again. I told my family and friends everything I'd experienced, but several of them didn't believe my stories, especially about moving up to the mountains during the day to escape the city. They all thought I was exaggerating. My brothers and Diina laughed at me when they saw me kneel to the floor and start to pray, the way my aunt had taught me. Now that I was back in Mogadishu and away from the awful unpredictability of Garbaharey, praying so often didn't seem as necessary, and after two days, I stopped.

I'd missed my friend Sarah while I was away, and we spent a lot of time together now that I was back. "I didn't think I'd see you again," Sarah admitted to me. "We heard that everyone in Garbaharey died."

I thought how strange it was that people had thought I was dead. I felt almost like a ghost, walking among the living again.

"I prayed to Allah that he would save you," Sara added. "And he did."

Now I felt lucky that I'd survived that unexpected air attack. But I was still worried about my aunt and thought about her all alone in that house, scared and with no one around to share the fear with. I wrote her many letters so she would know I hadn't forgotten her. Because I wasn't good at writing then, my brother Wali helped me and I, in return, washed his clothes. Wali and I would sit down at a table, and he would write down what I dictated. I would grow impatient with him because he'd write so slow. "Hurry up!" I told him, but he was a perfectionist and wanted to do proper work.

Slowly, the excitement of being at home wore away, and I started feeling guilty about leaving my aunt. I looked forward to the mail every day, hoping I would receive a letter from her. When I did get a letter or sometimes a package, she told me that people in Garbaharey were no longer afraid and were starting to walk outside in the daytime again, the way it had always been. She said I was welcome to visit her again the next time I had a holiday.

Despite hearing that Garbaharey was returning to normal, I wasn't sure I wanted to visit again so soon. As the days passed, I realized I was no longer the same person as I'd been before I visited my aunt. Something inside of me had changed. Now I slept a great deal and hesitated about playing outside. I grew distant, moody, and nervous. I might have left Garbaharey, but somehow, Garbaharey had followed me back home to Mogadishu. I couldn't forget the sound of the Ethiopian planes and the bombs and the earth trembling like the start of Judgment Day—and me hiding under the bed, praying for Allah to spare my life.

The Execution

One day when I was in the seventh grade, the entire school took an excursion to the city center to visit the seamen's school and the machine gun refinery. Before we left, we sang the national anthem and saluted the Somalian flag hoisted to the top of the pole for the daily flag ceremony. Four large buses arrived, picked us up, and drove us into town.

I don't remember much about the tours of the seamen's school and the gun refinery. What I remember most vividly is what happened afterward. We were taken into a courtyard that was used for military training, in a large open space near the sea. There were many soldiers in the square, several sailors, and a long row of posts. "What's going on?" a couple of students asked our teachers. "Why are we here?"

"You're going to witness an execution," one of the teachers said in a resigned voice.

An execution? My classmates and I looked at each other in confusion. Most of us did not understand how to react. Because I was so nervous, I started talking nonstop while standing as if glued to the side of my teacher, Fahan. She understood I was scared and explained what was going to happen.

"It's important for you to stay quiet, Qaali," Fahan said. She also sounded grim and serious. "All of you should stay quiet and calm. Don't make any noise while the execution is going on."

I stopped talking, as did the other children. The sight of the soldiers made me especially nervous because they reminded me of Garbaharey after the bombings. Suddenly, another twenty soldiers marched into the square, along with nine men who had their heads covered by red cloth bags. The men were tied to the posts while we all watched. The police and soldiers were guarding all points of access to the entire area to prevent relatives and friends of the condemned men from bombing the square to try and free them. Ten men in military uniforms and white caps separated us from the doomed men. These were the executioners. Led by a drum major, an orchestra began playing the Somalian national anthem about how strong President Siyaad Barre and if people made mistakes, they would face harsh punishments.

Finally, several generals arrived in a shiny jeep with several cars driving in front and behind them. There was a Somalian flag on the jeep. The generals emerged in their neat uniforms and lined up in front of the small crowd of onlookers. One of the generals, a handsome man with a short military-style haircut, held his hat in his hand as he explained that all Somalian citizens should understand that these men were guilty of the worst criminal activity— taking other people's lives.

Even after the general's speech, and even though I knew the accused men had done wrong, I still didn't want to see them executed. Time felt like it had slowed to a crawl. Although everyone in the crowd were black people, many of their faces were pale and stunned. A few had started to sweat. "Stand very still during the execution," the general said in a loud, clear voice.

"You're being monitored by the soldiers. If you move, we'll think you're trying to shoot at us, and we will respond."

Fahan and I looked at each other, stiffened, and let go of each other's hand. We didn't want to get shot. I glanced down at the ground, sick to my stomach. But no, I couldn't throw up. The soldiers might shoot me for that too.

I glanced back up in time to watch the firing squad aim and fire two or three shots each. The condemned men slumped against the poles and soldiers ran up to them to make sure they were dead. Then the bodies were quickly removed and placed into military trucks.

Suddenly, the ceremony and execution were over. The children ran, excited and curious, to the posts to which the executed men had been bound. Blood was splattered on the poles and the ground. *Are they dead?* I wondered. *Are they really dead?* I wrapped my arms around myself but still felt cold.

Fahan called us over and told us we would return to school now. Inside the bus, no one said a word. Fahan stared blankly in front of her. Normally, my classmates and I would tease each other and act totally wild, but today everyone felt strange and solemn. I wanted to return home to my family and talk about the execution. I didn't dare talk about it to anyone on the bus. I was afraid that if I said something wrong, I'd get executed next time.

As it turned out, the government had been experimenting with forcing students to witness an execution at a young age as a way of deterring them from committing crimes in the future. The parents were not informed about this in advance, nor were the teachers. When word got out and the newspaper reported the execution along with pictures of children as witnesses, some parents complained, and that experiment was quickly discontinued.

Life in my Family

When I was 12 years old, my mother was having a lot of financial problems. She didn't have a job, and she had a major fight with one of her brothers, who had been helping her financially and owned the house we lived in. After the fight, her brother no longer considered my mother a friend and told her she should move.

The house we moved into was in very poor condition. When it rained, water dripped in from the ceiling and through the walls. But we couldn't afford to rent a better place. There were only two rooms in this house. My brothers—Wali and Rush—slept in one room and a couple of my cousins also slept there when they visited us. All the boys shared two beds until my mother sent Wali and Rush to boarding schools because she could no longer afford to support them at home. In the other room, my mother, Diina and I shared a bed. Fortunately, our new neighbors were sweet, helpful, and tried to make us feel welcome. I was envious of the neighbor's children because they lived with both their parents, while I rarely saw my father, who was a nomad and lived far away.

I knew my mother had had a bad and contentious relationship with her own father. When my mother was a child, her father married a new wife every four to five years.

Once, when he married a new wife and she gave birth to two children, he threw her out and kept the children. My grandfather's sister and servants looked after all his kids. My grandfather hated women and had never wanted a daughter. He'd said if he ever had a daughter, he would bury her alive. My grandfather had nine sons with five different wives. My mother was the only daughter, and my grandfather never followed through on his threat to bury a daughter because he was serving as a mayor. To other people, my grandfather appeared a wise man and they loved him. No one other than family members knew the dark secret: he hated women and his own daughter. My mother wasn't allowed to enter the city because her father thought she would marry a strange man or become a whore. She grew up neglected, and because of this never learned to love anyone or fall in love. Yet as a young woman, she was beautiful and coveted. She married my father so she could escape her own father. She never truly loved my father, and eventually they were divorced. She never remarried and never forgave her parents or my father.

All of this influenced the way she raised me and my siblings. For example, my mother always ordered me to return straight home from school, just as her father had done with her. Other than going to school, I wasn't allowed to go outside the house without supervision. The same was true for Diina, while my brothers and male cousins were allowed the freedom to go into town whenever they pleased. I was envious of my brothers and thought it was unfair for my mother to not allow Diina and me the same privileges. My mother always said that Diina and I weren't allowed to go to town and meet boys because she was worried about us getting pregnant before we were married, but sometimes

I wondered if she was so strict because she didn't like me. Diina didn't care what our mother wanted, and she did as she pleased, often wearing perfume, and dressing up in smart clothes before going into town to meet up with friends. Usually, I was more obedient because I didn't like to contradict my mother. She always said that good girls stayed home with their families. On those rare occasions when I defied her orders and went into town anyway, she would call me a "whore" when I returned home and act coldly toward me. Now that she was the parent, my mother was treating me exactly as her father had treated her.

Sometimes I wanted to escape my mother's cruelty so badly that I invented lies to try and escape the house. Once I told her that I needed to go live with Aunt Halibo because she needed me and had no children to look after her in her old age. Another time, I asked my cousin Maryan if I could stay with her for a few weeks. Maryan agreed to this but only if I helped her watch over her three children after I returned from school. She had two boys and a girl. One of the boys was particularly hard to manage. Once, while I was watching over the children, the youngest boy was playing with a ball when he hit the pan of boiling water and the water fell on his hand and seriously burned him. Maryan got mad at me and sent me back to the volatile situation at home.

If home life wasn't bad enough with my mother, my relationship with Diina was difficult and stressful for years. Diina had been jealous of me since I was born. She was the third child with two older brothers, so she was used to being the youngest and the only girl. Everyone in the family pampered her. When Diina was three years old, I was born, and some of that attention shifted over to me.

Diina was not happy about it. Like my mother, Diina often showed her anger and resentment in violent ways. When I was two or three weeks old, Diina grew so jealous that she picked up a big knife and stabbed me in the leg, giving me a life-long scar. Another time, she pushed me into a bonfire and my face was burned. Whenever she was in a rage, she would hit my head, face, neck. There were times I was afraid she would kill me. She was also jealous that my brothers liked me and often protected me from her.

When I was older and physically stronger, I started to protect myself from her. Because Diina was so angry all the time, at my brothers and mother and especially me, my mother didn't know how to handle her, so my mother scolded me instead whenever there was a conflict with Diina. If Diina misbehaved, she often blamed what Diina had done onto me, and my mother would yell at me because it was easier to discipline me than Diina. For years Diina abused me, and everyone knew it, but my mother didn't want anyone outside the family to know, so nothing was ever done about Diina.

Since I was almost always at home, it was hard to make real friends. School was a haven for me. I talked and played with the other kids, but many of them were busy teasing and bullying each other, so I knew we were too different to become real friends. I daydreamed about a day when I could travel far from Mogadishu, see other countries, and have exciting adventures. I could escape the tension and strained relationships with my mother and Diina. I couldn't talk to my mother about things that interested me because she was so strict and critical. And even though my brothers were nice to me, I could tell they weren't interested in listening to me, either.

I missed my father a lot and often wished he would come and visit us, especially when my mother and I were fighting. I imagined that if my father were around, he would talk honestly to me, and I could find from him the care and love I wasn't getting from the rest of my family. But he never came. When I turned thirteen and one of my vacations approached, I finally persuaded my mother to allow me to visit him. This was difficult because my father and mother both hated each other and would not even greet one another if they crossed paths on a street in Baardheere. "Why do you want to visit a scum and a pig?" she asked me whenever I proposed a visit with my father. My mother had one stipulation before she would allow me to see my father: Diina had to come along with me.

I wasn't happy about spending any more time with Diina, but I knew my mother's mind was made up about this. My cousin's father drove Diina and me to see our father, who lived about 250 miles from Mogadishu. My cousin rode along with us, and my cousin and I laughed and sang the whole way while Diina sat quietly and stared out the window. Diina was older than my cousin and me and made it clear she found us childish and annoying.

Diina and I stayed with our aunt and cousins for about three weeks before our father came to pick us up. He was tall, lean, and handsome with long hair and striking white teeth. Yet our reunion with him felt awkward and insincere, since we hadn't seen him for so long and didn't really know each other well. Still, I liked his calm and his warmth, and he had more of a sense of humor than my mother had. Because my father was a nomad, he had no house of his own. He slept in a tent when he was outside tending to his animals. When

Diina and I were staying at my aunt's place, he came into town and slept with his sister.

My father's parents had been nomads, and they'd died before my father married my mother. I often wished that I'd had the opportunity to meet them or even just get to know them through pictures, but nomads didn't own cameras back then or have opportunities to get photographed. One of the first things Diina and I did with our father was visit their gravesites in the middle of a jungle. The graves were in a beautiful place surrounded by many fruit trees such as banana, blue dwarf palm, and moringa. The smell was so fragrant I felt like I was in a paradise garden. At one point I lay down in some nearby grass and stared up at the flowering trees and their small blue, yellow, and white flowers. Occasionally, I saw birds, large and small, in the trees. I didn't mind that the grass concealed lichen and snakes. When it was raining, the gravesite area smelled like strong fresh roses mixed with other wildflowers, and by sniffing that scent I felt that I got to know my grandparents a little better. My father had planted a mareer tree on the grave site so he could recognize the spot where his parents were buried. The tree had grown big and spacious and stood right above my grandmother's head. Twice a year the tree produced an orange fruit with a flavor that resembled sweet cherries. Some of the fruit from the tree had fallen to the ground and covered their graves. A wooden fence with my grandparents' names on it surrounded the graves. My father was very proud of the mareer tree as it stood vigil over his parents' graves.

My father was also proud of the cows and camels that he'd inherited from his father. He showed them to Diina and me. He kept the animals in the bush and on his parents' property that he'd also inherited. There was a lot of land where the animals could walk around and move freely. In the evenings, they were herded into a fenced area to protect them from lions and other predators during the night. My father owned several hundred camels, about fifty cows and thirty sheep, and a few white horses. I was able to pet the animals from time to time, but Diina didn't like them and mostly stayed far away. When she did get close to one of the animals, she plugged her nose and complained the animal smelled, and her behavior scared the animal and it usually backed away from her.

I loved looking after the cows. I wanted to milk them, but I couldn't figure out how to do it even though I tried several times. The cow udders felt hard, and when I pulled up and down on them, I must have done something wrong, because the cows moaned or balked. Once a cow got angry and kicked me, sending me and the milk bowl falling to the ground. A few nomad women were nearby and laughed, and I felt that I didn't belong in nomadic life if I couldn't milk a cow.

My father tried to teach me to milk a camel too, but that went even worse. The camels scared me. They were very tall and peed on their legs, and the pee smell was strong and vile. Whenever I stood next to a camel, I grew nervous and felt like I was standing next to an elephant. I also learned that male camels can be dangerous if you're not careful and don't know how to handle them. Once a camel, while begging for food, started chasing Diina and me. I liked baby camels and loved to watch them nursing their mothers. Camel mothers can also be dangerous if you touch their babies or handle them wrong. Once when I petted a baby camel with my fingernails, its fur soft and dirty, the mother camel grabbed me, and I fell at her feet. Fortunately, she didn't stomp on me. I never did learn how to milk either cows or camels, but I did learn how to feed them.

My father had a shepherd named Adam who looked after the cows and camels. Adam the Camel Shepherd was about thirty, a small, sweet, and shy man who had neither a wife nor children. He claimed he'd never been to a big city and had lived as a nomad his entire life. Often, I asked him questions about camels, like how old and how big they can get, and he would laugh pleasantly at my questions and answer them all. He told me other things as well, not just about camels. Once he took Diina and me to a small lake and pointed out where we could swim during the day. He also taught us where and how to find fruit and honey. Adam was much more present-minded than my father and had a seemingly calm and pleasant demeanor.

Adam loved all the animals but especially the camels. He loved the camels so much he named them and talked to them as if they were human. He tended to them when they were sick and intuitively could read if they needed anything. One of his biggest aims in life was to get as many camels as possible for himself. Getting married and having kids was secondary to owning camels.

After a few days, my father had to leave to spend some time in the bush with camels in a neighboring village, so Adam would take care of Diina and me for a full week. It was never clear to me exactly why my father had to be gone for so long, and later, when my mother found out about this, she accused my father of not bothering to spend time with Diina and me while we were visiting him. I didn't mind because I liked Adam, but Diina wasn't happy— she didn't like Adam or camels or my father's nomadic lifestyle. She wanted to go back and stay with our aunt, but I wanted to experience more of my father's lifestyle, and Diina knew it wasn't a good idea for us to separate, so we both stayed with Adam.

Despite Diina's reluctance, the first day under Adam's care went well. Diina and I got to know the camels' names. One of the camels had been named Qaali and another one Diina. There was an old female camel named Grandmother. But by the second day, Diina (my sister and not the camel) had grown unhappy again. She spent a lot of time sleeping under a tree and acting bored. She was accustomed to city life and already missed Mogadishu and her friends. She decided she not only didn't like the nomadic lifestyle, but also the food we were eating. There wasn't much food around other than camels' milk. Occasionally, Adam or I would find fruit or honey that we could eat in addition to drinking the camel milk. Diina didn't think she could live on camel's milk alone. She wanted bread, meat, rice, pasta, all the foods we were accustomed to back in Mogadishu.

One morning around lunchtime, Adam, Diina, and I were sitting under a dry tree beside a small lake because the temperature was so hot. Camels surrounded us, eating grass and wood. But Adam, Diina, and I had no food. Diina stared at the camels with a hungry look in her eye.

"Adam, you must slaughter a camel for us to eat," Diina said.

Almost instantly, Adam turned cold. Veins stood out in his forehead and neck. "No!" he snapped at Diina. "You're an evil witch. I don't like you."

Shocked, Diina started to cry. I was surprised at Adam's anger and a little scared. I realized I didn't know Adam very well and moved closer to Diina to comfort her. I sat down beside her and put my arms around her. "Everything will be okay," I said to her in a low voice so Adam couldn't hear. "Dad will come back soon, and if he doesn't come back, maybe we will have to go home and take a lift from the road."

Diina nodded, wiped her eyes, and touched my hair.

"It was all a big misunderstanding," I said, turning back to Adam.

Adam's behavior was still cold although he'd turned more reserved than angry.

"If you want meat and rice, all you have to do is go home," he said, looking straight at Diina.

The tension between Adam and Diina was palpable, and I was starting to think it wouldn't be a bad idea to go home early, even though I felt I still had much to learn about nomad life. "We have to stay with you until our father comes back," I told Adam.

Adam turned to me, and his eyes softened a little. "Then your sister should stop talking about slaughtering camels," he said.

I promised I wouldn't say another word about camels and nudged Diina to agree as well. Although she didn't dare mention camels again in front of Adam, she continued to walk around outside in short skirts and full makeup, as if she were still back in Mogadishu with an audience of boys, and she would complain loudly that her legs were getting cut from the prickly plants in the bush. Sometimes she would complain in front of Adam, and I feared he would grow upset again and yell at us, but he mostly ignored Diina after the camel incident. Diina also complained that it was my fault we were stuck out here in the bush without enough food to eat or a proper place to sleep, since I was the one who had wanted a chance to visit our father in the first place. I didn't want to spend time with Diina because she would blame me for something, and I wasn't comfortable hunting for fruit and honey with Adam the way I once had because I was afraid he might grow angry again. As a result, I spent more time wandering around by myself.

I was surprised by how many snakes were around the area where my father lived. They were everywhere and you couldn't help but see them, slithering in the grass or hanging from trees. One day when I was out alone and exploring the bush, I ran across a huge python eating a small deer. I stared, transfixed, both fascinated and frightened. Then I ran back to Adam and told him what I had seen.

"You shouldn't be walking around alone," he told me with a small smile. "Those big snakes could eat a child."

After that, I stayed close to the camels.

When my father finally returned from the village, Diina ran to him immediately, sobbing. "What has happened, my girl?" my father asked.

I glanced over at Adam, who looked nervous about what Diina was going to say to our father.

"Adam wasn't nice to us," she said. "He treated us badly. He didn't give us any food and we had to drink milk the whole time. You should fire him."

"Now, now," my father said and glanced over at Adam. I saw them smile quietly at each other and then my father asked Adam how the camels had been. I couldn't help but notice that my father asked about the camels but not about Diina and me.

"When you're a nomad, you rarely eat meat and bread," my father explained to Diina once he'd heard the update about the camels. "It's too hard to get those things."

I wondered why our father had never prepared Diina and me for having so little to eat while out in the bush, but I didn't say anything. When he turned to me and asked how I had been, I simply said, "Fine. It's been nice."

Diina stared at me like I'd betrayed her. "You're stupid!" she said to me. "You have no idea what was going on."

I didn't argue with her because I didn't want her to hit me. Again, Diina suggested that our father should fire Adam, but it was clear to me that my father wouldn't do it. Adam and my father were close friends, and I doubted my father could ever fire him. And the truth was, I didn't want Adam fired. Despite his flashes of anger, I found him exciting. He knew how to do so many things that Diina and I could not do. Not only was he good at taking care of camels, but he'd also taught me how to find food in the bush and survive out in the wild. He knew which animals were dangerous to humans and which ones weren't. Adam had also taken me out into the heath to show me elephants and zebras. He was a real nomad who had been single his entire life and rarely saw women. Nomads have unwritten rules, such as that you may not steal or rape someone, and most nomads keep these rules. If a nomad rapes a girl, he's not allowed to stay in the area because everyone would grow scared of him. That's one reason there aren't many crimes in the world of the nomads.

In Somalia, everyone is a Muslim. People take Fridays off and have parties and visit each other. One Friday, my father said he'd take Diina and me to a small nomad camp nearby because there was going to be a party. Adam would stay and take care of the camels and other animals. I was excited to go, but Diina was more reluctant. She thought nomads were dirty and uninteresting and the only thing she wanted was to return to Mogadishu. Sometimes I wanted to return to Mogadishu as well, but I also could see the advantages of being a nomad. Diina and I had freedom here we didn't have at home. For one, our mother would never have invited us to a party. Finally, Diina decided to go along with our father and me. She didn't want to be left alone with the animals and Adam, and she was so bored that any distraction was welcome.

On Friday afternoon, my father and Diina and I all went to a small town nearby, where one of my uncles, Abdullahi, lived. His daughter, Cadeey, was the same age as me. She was very tall and beautiful, with long hair and a graceful neck, and her large, expressive eyes gave her the look of a photo model. All the nomad boys loved her. If I went to the party with her, I thought, I'd probably get a lot of attention. We all had dinner with my uncle, and at nine o'clock, Cadeey and I went to the nomad camp where the party was being held. My father decided he was too old for the party and wanted to stay and visit with my uncle and his family. Diina claimed she had no interest in a "bush party" and decided to stay behind with our father and read an Indian love novel while hiding away in one of my uncle's huts.

The road Cadeey and I took to the party wound through the bush and was very dark. It was rainy and there were strange noises and small animals everywhere. The rain was warm, and I didn't mind that my hair and clothes were getting soaked. But I was very scared of snakes because I'd seen so many different kinds around the area where my father lived. Suddenly, the unfamiliarity of this place—the dark path, the sound of the animals—scared me so much that I froze in place.

"I can't go on," I said. "I want to go back."

"No," Cadeey said firmly, rain dripping down her face. "You can't go back alone. You should experience a full nomad party."

After we'd walked nearly two miles, we finally reached the party. A large bonfire had been lit far away from the tents and everyone was gathered around the fire. As Cadeey and I approached the crowd, I saw people from the ages of fourteen to around forty. Most of the people were single. Cadeey and I joined the throng of women who were watching the men dance. We stood in a long line, singing and clapping. I tried to clap in rhythm with the rest of the women but found it difficult. I also wanted to dance but knew that women were not allowed to dance, just the men. The women were living in a man's world and that's just the way it was. Still, I was enjoying myself as I tried to imitate the other women. At one point, I was smiling so hard that my mouth hung open. Cadeey nudged me and whispered that women weren't supposed to smile so much or look at the men too hard. I closed my mouth quickly.

When we'd been clapping in line for over an hour, a man approached us. He was a tall and handsome man who danced beautifully. It was clear by the way he stared at Cadeey that he was attracted to her. I watched him warily as he stood in front of Cadeey and me. Suddenly, he pulled out a dagger and started cutting his arm. I backed away, horrified. I thought he was going to kill someone. I ran off toward the trees and shouted for help. People stared at me as I dashed past. "What happened to her?" I heard someone say, and someone else said, "Is she okay?" Because it was so dark and I was so pumped up with adrenaline, I ran straight into a tree and hurt my shin. I cried out, startled and in pain.

Cadeey rushed up behind me and touched my shoulder. "Qaali, don't be scared," she said, panting and out of breath. "It's normal what that man did. Nomad men cut themselves with their daggers to show us women that he's strong and not afraid of anything."

I was comforted by what Cadeey said, and grateful that she was protecting me like a big sister would, a way that Diina never acted with me. I bent over and looked at my shin, which was now bleeding. I was embarrassed that I'd panicked and had perceived the man as a threat. I glanced apologetically at Cadeey, but I could see that she thought it was strange I'd gotten scared and had run off like that. "Come back now," she said.

Three young men who were about eighteen years old walked over to us. I couldn't see their faces clearly because it was so dark, but I knew they had followed us from the party. "Do you need help?" they asked.

"No, thanks," Cadeey said. "We're fine."

But the men remained where they were, staring at us and laughing a little. My eyes had adjusted somewhat to the dark, so I could see that they were focused mostly on Cadeey. Still, I was embarrassed that I'd hurt myself and that there was blood on my right shin. "Sorry," I muttered to Cadeey.

We returned to the party, and I rejoined the line and started clapping again even though I didn't know what the party was about. I noticed a few people staring at me. They probably thought I was sick in the head or handicapped in some way for screaming and running off the way I had.

Eventually, as the night wore on, Cadeey grew annoyed with me. She wasn't used to spending time with a city girl like me, any more than I was used to her culture.

She said she thought I was childish. "I don't want to take care of you all the time," she told me.

I was upset that she saw me as an intrusion and felt she needed to babysit me. I wanted to join the party and talk to other people, but I felt like a stranger even though my father was known throughout the area. I didn't feel like I would meet anyone else unless I stayed close to Cadeey.

On the way home, two men from the party who knew Cadeey came up to walk home with us. I couldn't see their faces very well because it was too dark, but I could tell they weren't the same two guys who had followed Cadeey and me when I ran off from the party. One of the men started talking to Cadeey while the other talked to me. He said his name was Gelle, and even though it was dark, I could see he was slender, gentle, and attractive. I guessed he was about seventeen years old or even older. He wanted to know more about Mogadishu, how big it was and what the houses looked like, since he'd never been to a large city. He also told me more about the nomad lifestyle.

Gelle and his friend followed us all the way home. My father, uncle, and Diina were already in bed. Gelle and I sat down on the ground and talked some more while we waited for Cadeey and her suitor, who had disappeared behind some bushes.

"I'm looking for my future wife," Gelle told me bluntly. "I'm pretty rich. I have a lot of camels." He stared down at the ground when he talked to me and seemed nervous. I knew he was uncomfortable and felt stuck with me while his friend was with Cadeey. "I can afford a wife," he added.

I glanced away, unsure what to say. I'd never had a boy talk to me about finding a wife. "I thought a nomad could only take another nomad as a wife," I said.

Gelle shook his head. "That's not always true," he said.

"Then it's possible for me to marry a nomad." My heart began to beat more quickly as I said this. "But my father would like to get a lot of camels from my future husband."

"How many does he want?"

"Fifteen camels who are fifteen years old," I said, free and easy.

Gelle laughed so loudly I was afraid he'd wake up my father and uncle. I smiled back at him uncertainly. Why was everyone laughing at me tonight? "I can manage that," he said. Then he mentioned he had to leave soon, but he'd like to stop by the next day and visit me again so we could continue this conversation.

I wondered if this was what it was like to have a boyfriend. I'd never had a boyfriend before. At the same time, I knew Gelle wasn't interested in me. To him, I was still a little girl. A boy was forbidden to date a girl under fifteen years old. "What time are you coming?" I asked.

He shrugged and said he wasn't sure. "How about 8:00 at night," I suggested.

Gelle explained that nomadic appointments followed different schedules than appointments made by city people. "I'd rather come at 1:00 a.m." he said.

I was surprised by his suggestion and thought it odd for a stranger, a young man, to want to come and wake me up in the middle of the night. "No, I can't do that," I said. "It's too late."

We smiled at each other even though we understood our date was cancelled and there was no agreement between us. Then Cadeey and the other man walked over to us, and Gelle and I said goodbye to each other.

When I woke up the next morning, my father and Uncle Abdullahi were sitting on a couple of chairs, drinking tea. Cadeey was out fetching water in town, and Diina was still in one of the cabins, reading her Indian love novel, paging through Russian picture magazines, and hiding from the sun. My father and uncle looked at me with amusement and laughed when they said good morning to me. "Qaali, I'm embarrassed you can't figure out how old a camel gets," my father said. "A fifteen-year-old camel is old and costs next to nothing. The best camel is between three and five years old."

I felt myself blush. "Why are you asking me that?" I said, even though I thought I knew why. Last night he'd probably overheard my conversation with Gelle and was surprised at my ignorance about camels and nomadic life.

The day before Diina and I went back to spend more time at our aunt's house, we grilled meat out in the bush with my father. He slaughtered a young camel for us because he knew we wanted to eat meat. He dug a large hole and filled it with dry wood. Then he took a stick, placed it on a piece of dry wood and quickly rubbed the stick between his hands until it started to burn. Soon we had a full fire. We put small pieces of meat on sticks and lay the meat into the fire. After some time, my father put glowing coals down into the hole and placed the rest of the camel meat there as well. I was impressed that my father knew how to do all of this. Both Diina and I enjoyed the camel meat and the last evening with our father, but it was probably good that Adam the Camel Shepherd wasn't there with us.

Uncle Adam

My Uncle Adam was a general under the autocratic Siyaad Barre presidency. He was kind and loving when he came to visit us, and my brothers and Diina and I loved him. Since we didn't have a lot of contact with our father, Uncle Adam did his best to help take care of us when he was around. Unlike my mother, he listened to us when we wanted to talk, seemed genuinely interested in our company, and frequently gave us gifts. He was also a strong and stubborn man who did not change his mind readily, and so working under the command of Siyaad Barre did not suit him.

Although Uncle Adam and Siyaad Barre came from the same clan and had grown up in the same city, there was a constant power struggle between them. Siyaad Barre had posted my uncle to work several times in various dangerous and strife-ridden areas of Somalia. My uncle was convinced Siyaad Barre did this because he hoped that Uncle Adam would get killed at some point. But Uncle Adam was both shrewd and lucky and always returned unscathed.

Still, Uncle Adam was jailed several times for his political disagreements with Barre. My uncle wanted to end the clan wars between the north and south in Somalia.

He also wanted to stop the war between Ethiopia and Somalia. He favored becoming allies with the United States and Europe in the Cold War and did not approve of Barre aligning with Russia and communism. Barre spent a vast amount of money waging war in Ethiopia, which led to high unemployment and a poor economy, which fueled the civil war between north and south in Somalia. Uncle Adam could see all these problems linked to Barre and so was opposed to much of Barre's political agenda. But Barre was afraid that if he was forced to step down, my uncle, a strong and charismatic leader, would take over.

I remember one day when my siblings and I visited Uncle Adam in a special prison, the so-called "underground prison," which was located roughly 22 miles from Mogadishu. My mother didn't come with us since she and my father were divorced, and she didn't consider herself part of my father's family. But she didn't mind if the rest of us went to visit, since she thought Uncle Adam was a role model for us because of his government job. To get to the prison, you had to go to a small house surrounded by construction work and walk down some stairs to the prison below. Only political dissidents of Sayaad Barre were placed in this prison. My uncle believed the prison was secretly funded by Russians.

The prison was cold, humid, and murky from poor quality lights. Once we were checked in by some guards, we were shown to a visiting room. When we saw Uncle Adam inside the room, we all began to cry. Even my uncle looked on the verge of tears. I was glad to see that at least he wasn't handcuffed. I shook his hand and sat on a chair in front of him, and my brothers and sister did as well. We asked him when he'd be able to come home and he said soon, but he couldn't say exactly when that would be. All the while we were talking, grim-looking guards with guns stood nearby, so we couldn't ask Uncle Adam anything too personal or political. I still didn't understand why Uncle Adam was in prison. He'd worked for the government for thirty years and had extensive experience in politics. But we also knew what our mother had told us: Uncle Adam would eventually get imprisoned or even executed if he didn't flee the country.

"Don't worry," Uncle Adam said, trying to reassure us. "When I do come home, we're going to have a big party."

Finally, he was released from prison right around Ramadan, after months of living in the cold and dark underground. When Ramadan was over, he threw a huge party for family and friends, as promised. Uncle Adam didn't dare invite neighbors because he was afraid that they might be working for the government. Before Uncle Adam went to jail, he'd lived in a large white villa that was owned by the government. Once he was imprisoned, he lost the house and all the services that went along with it. Now that he was out of prison, he was living in a small house. There wasn't enough space in the house to fit the many guests, so a lot of people were standing and sitting outside and in the garden.

The party began at nine in the morning and didn't end until eleven o'clock at night. His wife served an endless supply of hot food and drinks. People came and went as they pleased, and there was always a steady stream of people coming and going. During the party, Uncle Adam looked so strong, kind, and happy. He came over to talk to me several times, in his newly pressed clothes and expensive perfume, and each time gave me a big hug. I was fourteen years old at that point and deeply fascinated by him and his work with the government. I wanted to ask him about the rumors I'd heard about the government—that after his imprisonment he had become friends with Barre again. But he was usually surrounded by other people, and a convenient opportunity to ask him never arose. I followed my uncle with my eyes as he walked around greeting people and shaking their hands, sometimes engaging them in long and spirited conversation. Even if I could get Uncle Adam's attention long enough to talk to him, would he even answer my questions? After all, I was a teenaged girl, and in Somalia young girls weren't supposed to talk politics. We were supposed to be cute, neat, and pleasant, without strong opinions of our own. I found myself growing frustrated and unable to relax and enjoy the party. When I went home at eight o'clock, I wasn't happy with the way the day had gone. I wished I had asked Uncle Adam about his current relationship with Barre.

Four months later, Uncle Adam threw a second party. By then I'd forgotten my disappointment with his first party and was happy to be invited to another one. Everyone dressed up for the party and gathered once again at Uncle Adam's house. In the middle of the party, Uncle Adam stood up in front of his guests and gave a speech. He said he'd like to hold a holiday in his lovely birthplace, Bardere. "If anyone would like to join me, you will be welcome," he said, holding his large black glasses in his hand. Barre also wore large black glasses. "I have a Land Rover and a truck, so there's room for a lot of people."

After Uncle Adam finished his speech, I was one of the first people who went over to him. "I'd like to go along, if you don't mind," I said, even though I hadn't checked with my mother yet to get her permission.

My uncle smiled and patted my shoulder. "You're always welcome, Qaali," he said.

There were two more months to wait before the school holidays started, but I was already looking forward to my departure. For once, I was diligent about doing my homework and the housework, because I was so excited about the upcoming trip, and I was grateful that my mother had agreed to let me take the trip with Uncle Adam, so I wanted to make her happy. I cleaned the house and did most of the shopping because my mother hated shopping, especially in hot weather. Baardheere was roughly 185 miles from Mogadishu, so it would take an entire day and maybe more to get there, due to the rough and bumpy roads. But the distance didn't matter to me. In fact, the further away from Mogadishu a city was, the more exciting it seemed.

Finally, the day came for us to leave. We were scheduled to be gone for a month. I'd washed and ironed my clothes and polished my shoes. I'd packed four bags filled with clothes and shoes, as if I were intending to move away for good. My brothers and Diina thought I was crazy for packing so much, and they shook their heads as they smiled at me.

Uncle Adam drove me to Baardheere along with three of my cousins—two girls, Halimo and Cadeey, and one boy, Hamsa. All three of my cousins were older than me, but that didn't matter. I could talk to them about anything. With Halima and Cad, we talked a lot about clothes. Their clothes were nicer than mine, and I was envious of the purple dresses they wore. They also wore fancy perfume from Paris and not Somalia. Halima had a shiny pair of saddle shoes from Rome that I also admired. Halima and Cad treated me both like their little sister and as someone who was their own age.

As much as I liked Halima and Cad, I was closest to Hamsa, who was four years older than me and extremely funny. But he was also small and very fragile, with one leg shorter than the other so he looked a little crooked. He lived at the university and was wise for his age. He read a lot of books including philosophy. He had access to foreign magazines and sometimes gave me a few of them, with pictures of far-off cities like New York City, London, and Paris. On the drive to Baardheere, he entertained us by singing badly and making weird faces, so we were always in fits of laughter. We also had to stop along the way several times so that Hamsa could dash out of the car and pee behind a bush.

Uncle Adam's wife owned the house we stayed in while in Baardheere. It had four rooms and a lovely garden where we sat outside and lingered in the evening. Uncle Adam and Hamsa slept in one of the rooms, and Halima, Cad, and I slept in another room. My cousins and I would lie awake in our beds at night and whisper until three in the morning. Sometimes Uncle Adam would step into the room in his pajamas and ask us, "When are you all going to sleep?"

Our answer was the same every time. "We're on vacation," we said. "Does it make any difference when we sleep?"

He would just shake his head at us and leave the room.

During the day, several men often came around to visit Uncle Adam. They sat out in the garden, drank tea, smoked a lot of cigarettes, and chewed khat to get high.

Then they talked a lot about Barre's government and the increasing unrest going on in the community. I only half-listened to what they said but got the sense things were not going well and that people were becoming increasingly frustrated with Barre.

While on vacation, I learned that once a year, a large summer party was held in the neighboring town of Fafahdun. Many people in the area, I was told, took off a full week from work to attend, although it was not a religious party. Camels, cows, chickens, goats, and lambs were all slaughtered and served as food for the many guests. Halima, Cad, and I wanted to go to the party, so Uncle Adam's driver, Abdi, agreed to drive us there. He was a nice, somewhat quiet young man. He liked us because we treated him like our brother instead of an employee.

Hamsa decided not to join us because he preferred to stay in Baardheere and meet with the mayor, where he would discuss politics, governmental policy, and social problems. I was impressed how mature Hamsa was for his age and how much he wanted to make a difference in the community. Uncle Adam had an important meeting with some senior generals and couldn't attend the party as well. Halima, Cad, and I were disappointed that he couldn't join us, and I could tell that Uncle Adam wasn't very enthusiastic about having to attend the government meeting. He told us to take good care of ourselves, enjoy the party, and he would come along with Abdi in four days to pick us up.

Abdi drove us to Fafahdun and then returned to Baardheere so he could drive my uncle to his meeting at a large military base in Baidoa. The day after we arrived and the day before the party, Halima, Cad, and I got together with other young people from the area to climb a small mountain. I wasn't prepared for the physical exertion of the climb. Even after four hours of hiking uphill, we still hadn't reached the top. I was hot and my T-shirt was soaked with sweat. Occasionally I felt dizzy because we were climbing so high, and I had a fear of heights. Once I froze and screamed when we were halfway up. I couldn't help myself; my fear of falling was too strong. I was afraid to continue forward and afraid to turn back. My cousins encouraged me to keep moving, and eventually I got control of my fear and continued to follow them up.

Despite the heat and my fear of heights, I enjoyed the striking views and the many fruit trees that were in bloom, mostly Dheen and Goosi, which are wild fruit trees found in the bush. We ate a lot of fruit and drank the water we had brought with us. Because it was the rainy season, everything was green, lush, and fragrant. We came across a large group of monkeys, some standing in the trees and others on rocks, and the male monkeys shouted what sounded like "huu, huu." I'd seen monkeys in the city, and they were always cute and friendly, but monkeys in the bush were aggressive and dangerous. At one point some of the monkeys ran toward me, baring their long yellow teeth. Terrified, I turned and ran away from them. Some of the people in our group laughed at me. "Don't look scared," they said. "Shout back at them."

I picked up a stone and shouted, and soon the monkeys quieted down and walked calmly back into the jungle.

Another important thing my cousins and I learned from the other young people on that hike was the importance of brushing our teeth. After each meal, we should brush our teeth, they told us, and they didn't recommend using an ordinary toothbrush. They said we should brush our teeth with a small, fresh twig from a caday tree. When we all returned to town, I became aware that the teeth of the villagers were much whiter than ours. In Mogadishu, I'd always used plastic toothbrushes while my mother bought the caday twigs on the street. Now I wondered if my mother had been right all along, and I should start using the twigs as well. I promised myself that I would start brushing my teeth four times a day instead of just twice. My cousins and I made a pact that we would stay away from sweets as much as possible once we got home from vacation. We all wanted to have teeth as white and impressive as the people of Fafahdun.

The next day, the party was well underway when my cousins and I arrived. The townspeople were friendly and hospitable, and Halima, Cad, and I enjoyed the attention we received for being out of town. In the afternoon, a large amount of food was served—Indian rice, flat white bread, salad, assorted meat, and fruits including mango and watermelon. The food was laid out on large buffet tables with white tablecloths so people could help themselves. Every now and then, a waiter would pass by with trays of tea, dates, and juice. After people had finished eating, they began to dance the village dance—women moving around swivelling their hips and men jumping up and down and singing a love song. We also met several members of our family there, including my Aunt Gelo and her daughter Jad. I didn't know my aunt and Jad very well, so it was nice to run into them again at the party.

When we'd been in Fafahdun for three days, Abdi returned. Halima, Cad, and I were sitting outside the house when he arrived. He looked sad and downcast as he walked toward us, slowly and uncertainly. I felt the first hint of dread; something wasn't right. We were supposed to have another day in Fafahdun, and Uncle Adam was supposed to join Abdi when he came to pick us up. I glanced over at my cousins and saw the same look of dread and suspicion on their faces.

Halima, Cad, and I hurried over to Abdi and started asking questions all at once, our voices spilling over each other:

"Where is our father?"

"Where is Uncle Adam?"

"What's going on, is anything the matter?"

Abdi raised his hand to indicate we should be quiet, then he glanced around to see if anyone was within hearing range. "Let's go inside," he said.

My cousins and I followed him into the house. Now I was certain something was wrong. I felt dizzy and there was a dull ringing in my ears.

"I have to tell you something," he said in a grave voice. "Don't cry out loud and ruin the village party."

Halima, Cad, and I sat down and stared quietly at Abdi as he told us that Uncle Adam had been killed the day before. He'd gone to his meeting, and as soon as he'd climbed into the car to drive away, he'd been shot several times. Another car had pulled up beside Uncle Adam's car, a soldier had stepped out and shot my uncle, then hurried back into the car and drove away. Apparently, the man who shot Uncle Adam worked at the same office where my uncle had his meeting. This was, Abdi believed, a clear case of a political assassination.

Halima, Cad, and I shook our heads in stunned silence. "I don't believe you," Halima said, and Cad and

I agreed with her. We were too shocked and stunned to believe what Abdi was saying.

"Of course, it's true," Abdi said. "I was sitting at the wheel when they shot him three times in the head. I was lucky I wasn't hit."

Finally, my cousins and I could no longer deny the truth. We wailed in grief, clutching each other's hands for comfort, forgetting that we'd promised Abdi we'd be quiet so as not to spoil the party. The shock was so great I nearly passed out. Everything blurred around me.

My cousins and I packed our bags and drove away from Fafahdun without saying goodbye to all the people who had been so kind to us, giving us food and a place to stay. We were all silent in the car, too dazed to talk or eat. We picked up Hamsa in Baardheere, and then we asked Abdi to drive us straight back to Mogadishu. Hamsa cried several times and stared out the car window or down at the floor in stunned disbelief that his father had been assassinated. Abdi took some breaks along the way and smoked a little while the rest of us sat in the car, miserable and unmoving. I still couldn't grasp that Uncle Adam had been murdered and I would never see him again. After we'd arrived in Mogadishu and my cousins had climbed out of the car, I asked Abdi to drive me home. I knew that a lot of people would soon arrive at my uncle's house to cry and share memories of him, and I didn't know if I could bear it. I just wanted the company of my own family.

The house was unusually quiet when I arrived home, even though several family members were present, not just my mother and siblings but also a few cousins and other relatives. Some had gathered in the kitchen while others were standing out on the balcony or in the garden. When my mother saw me, she said, "Hello, it's good that you came right home."

No one said anything else because they were so upset. Occasionally, I heard someone muttering a prayer on Uncle Adam's behalf. Some people cried while others stood silent and glum, lost in their thoughts. Diina was almost crazy with grief. She walked through the house crying loudly, occasionally slamming doors or swearing at people for no reason. Once she flung herself on the floor and started wailing. Diina had been especially close to Uncle Adam and considered him a father figure.

I had brought no gifts home with me, nor did we talk about what I had experienced during the holiday. My uncle's body was transported by helicopter to Mogadishu, where he was to be buried a few days later. His body was kept frozen at a large hospital because the government wanted to investigate his death, even though there were rumors that Barre himself had arranged to have Uncle Adam assassinated.

I hadn't said goodbye to Uncle Adam because I'd thought we'd see him again in four days. Fortunately, I'd managed to ask my uncle all the questions I'd been wanting to ask him since his party after he was released from prison. He'd explained to me that everyone who held positions in the government took money from the country's coffers to build houses and buy large cars for themselves. Everyone who worked under Siyaad Barre had become rich and had no respect for either the president or the citizens. People in Somalia were always told it was Barre's fault that the country's economy was going downhill, and that unemployment was rising. Because so many citizens didn't like or trust Barre's government and regarded him as a dictator, it was easy to get them to believe it was Barre who was taking money from the government back accounts. But according to my uncle, the real picture was quite a different one. I'd asked Uncle Adam why he had such problems with the government, and he mentioned the corruption, the high unemployment, the way Barre's government was not working on behalf of the people.

"It's hard," Uncle Adam told me. "Siyaad Barre and I are from the same clan, and I'm friends with many of the others sitting in power right now." Then, smiling down at me, he added, "You don't have to worry about me. I'll be okay."

Sara

Not long after my Uncle Adam's death, I was invited to a housewarming party at Sara's parents' new multi-story house near the Indian Ocean. When Sara and her family had lived next door to us, they'd lived in an ordinary single-family house and driven around a small, old Italian car. It wasn't until Sara's father became a local bank director that the family's financial fortunes changed dramatically. Just a few months after his new job, Sara's father bought a new Mercedes and some coastal land. A year later, the entire family moved to the mansion by the ocean.

When I arrived at the housewarming, there were many shiny and fancy cars already parked along the driveway. At the front door, I rang the doorbell and the door swung open automatically. I laughed, excited, and stepped into the house, which was huge. It was probably easy to see that I'd never been inside such a nice house before. My eyes were wide as I stared at the wicks, the high ceilings, the ornate furniture. Several people were standing nearby, most of them young, wealthy, and dressed in expensive clothes, and they laughed at my reaction to the house. I was annoyed by their laughter and stares. Already I could see these were bourgeoise people who viewed me as a girl from the bush stumbling into their fancy party.

I walked to a door leading out into a garden and saw Sara talking to several people I didn't know. When she saw me standing in the doorway, she walked over and gave me a little hug. She looked different from the Sara who had been my neighbor. Now Sara looked elegant and fashionable, wearing an expensive white dress from Paris, a pair of high heels, and Chanel No. 5 perfume. Her normally curly hair was now smooth and piled high on her head. "Wow, you look wonderful," I told her.

At the same time, I was growing self-conscious. I was wearing a yellow dress which I considered nice, but it was inexpensive and made in Mogadishu, not Paris. The cheap perfume I was wearing I'd stolen from Diina, and the small gold necklace I wore was also Diina's. My pair of brown saddle shoes looked clumsy next to the sleek shoes of her other guests. Other than me, all of Sara's guests were rich young people, and I was reminded, again, of how much I didn't fit in with this crowd of glamour and money. I also noticed the difference in Sara, not only in how she looked but how she acted. Sometimes she spoke with an affected British accent. I felt the class difference between us, dividing us. We didn't know quite what to say to each other.

Sara showed me around outside, pointing out the huge swimming pool out in the garden that was surrounded by squawking parrots and chattering monkeys.

When she was finished giving me the tour, she asked what I thought about the house. "It's wonderful!" I exclaimed, still daunted by the opulence of everything.

Sara told me she had a whole apartment for herself at the back end of the house, and that was where the teens were gathering while the adults congregated in the living room. We hurried off to Sara's apartment. The room was crowded with teenagers. Michael Jackson songs were being played, and I couldn't help but notice that all the young guys had hairstyles that resembled Michael Jackson's. All the girls in the room were dressed in the same way as Sara, in smart and showy clothes. Some were even wearing diamond rings. Many of the girls glanced over at me with downcast eyes; some of them smirked in a condescending way. Only a few said "hello" in a low voice, and then they turned away so they wouldn't have to start a conversation.

Sara pointed me to a table where a variety of drinks were laid out—red, yellow, and blue juice as well as Coca-Cola and Fanta. I knew three girls at the party because they went to the same school I did, but they were too busy talking with the rich young people to bother with me. They seemed surprised to see me at Sara's party. As I glanced around the room, I saw the arrogant looks on most of their faces, and the way they glared at me and made it clear without saying a word that they didn't think I belonged there. After a short time, I wandered away, feeling awkward and uncomfortable.

I wandered around the garden for a while, looking at the festive party decorations. Sara's new friends came from rich, well-known, and well-connected families. I knew I was different from them, invisible and lonely because I didn't have the money or live in the luxury that most of them did. Up until a short time ago, Sara hadn't either. I was confused where all her family's money had come from that allowed them to make such a dramatic change in lifestyle. I wondered this even more when Sara found me in the garden and asked me, "Guess where I'm going on vacation?"

"Where?"

"Paris!" she exclaimed. "Can you believe it?"

Later, Sara took me to see the new Toyota her father had bought for her. She also had her own personal driver. I shook my head in disbelief. Now I couldn't stand keeping quiet any longer. "How can you afford all of this?" I asked.

"My father's a bank director," she said in a lofty voice. "You know that. All the money comes from the bank where he works."

"How much does he make? To afford all of this?"

Sarah shrugged and looked away, as if she didn't care for my questions. "I don't know about that," she said. "Maybe he borrowed it from the bank."

I didn't ask any more questions, but I was worried about how much Sara's world had changed and wondered if our friendship could survive now that she was so wealthy, and I wasn't. Maybe she would lose interest in me if I wasn't a beautiful and rich girl.

A few months later, in 1986, my family prepared to move again, this time to another house further away from the city center. The house was bigger, nicer, and cheaper, and my mother was offered the house by the government and couldn't pass it up. I was about to start high school and wasn't thrilled to have to change schools and leave my best friends. One evening shortly before our move, I was sitting in the kitchen and helping my mother make supper. My big brother Rush was coming home for a visit, and we were looking forward to seeing him, so my mother and I were preparing his favorite dish, lamb meat with curry rice.

Once Rush had arrived and we were sitting down for supper, I dared to ask my mother a question I'd been thinking about for a few days. "Instead of moving to the new house, do you think I could go live with Sara instead?" I asked.

Although my relationship with Sara had changed since she'd grown wealthy and snobbish, I thought staying with her was still preferable than moving to a new school and risk getting bullied and having no friends. Living with Sara would also help me escape my mother's control, which was becoming intolerable to me. I was hopeful that Rush would agree with me and help persuade my mother.

Instead, my brother shook his head adamantly. "Bad idea," he said with a frown. He took a bite of the chicken curry. "You are a little girl of fifteen who has a good family supporting you. Why would you want to go live with a friend?"

"I don't want to lose my friends and start a new school again. Sara thinks it's a good idea. They live in a big house now and have a lot of rooms and servants. I wouldn't have to work and could focus on school and homework."

"I agree with your brother," my mother said. I could see in her eyes that she was angry and would never agree to my proposal. "How will you cope without your family? You could get pregnant or marry a poor man before you are ready."

"But none of that will happen if I'm living with Sara! Her father and brothers will protect me."

Rush said he still thought it was a bad idea. "If you get pregnant and need to marry early, you'll have to manage on your own," he warned me. "We won't be able to take care of you anymore."

"That's the end of this crazy discussion!" my mother yelled. "You will stay with me in the new house!"

Rush glanced at me from across the table and communicated with his eyes that I should drop the subject. I knew then my battle was lost. "Okay, I understand you," I said quietly so I wouldn't make matters worse.

Despite my disappointment that I couldn't live with Sara and that I was going to have to move away from my friends, the new move had one strong advantage: I got to have my own bedroom, a small, dark room located at the back of the house. I was so excited and proud of my new room that I wanted to show it off to everyone, both boys and girls. But my mother insisted that I couldn't have friends in my room, even girls. Still, I was happy that I had a room of my own, where I could hide away for some privacy whenever I wanted.

Even with my own room and with more privacy, I continued to lose weight from the stress of not getting along with my mother. Often, I felt I couldn't live with her anymore. She lacked empathy and self-control. Even after all these years, she hadn't gotten any better at speaking normally and was still raising her voice or shouting. Often, she thought about herself and her own needs over those of her children. She'd had Rush when she was nineteen, still nearly a child herself, and so didn't know much about being a good mother. She couldn't cook well and had not learned proper housekeeping in her childhood. I was a sensitive child, so her anger and occasional violence rattled me. I avoided her as much as possible, and as a result, we didn't have much of a relationship. I lived with her because I had to, but I was waiting for the day I was an adult and had finished school, and then I could move away the same way my older siblings had.

Soon, I came up with another idea about how to live away from my mother before I was an adult. Without her knowledge, I applied to a free boarding school owned by the government. The boarding school was eighteen miles from Mogadishu and accepted both boys and girls. After the summer break, I received an acceptance letter in the mail. I was thrilled at the thought of going to this school and living away from home. Maybe since this offer involved school, my mother would be more receptive to the idea than she'd been to the idea of me moving in with Sara's family.

However, no one in my family thought the boarding school was a good idea, either. Since all my siblings had gone to school in the traditional way, everyone assumed that was the way I should do it, too. One day, my mother came into my room to tell me that I would be starting at the local high school in a week. As usual, she was unsmiling and seemed annoyed and impatient.

I didn't know how to convince her or anyone in my family to let me attend the boarding school. Defeated, I simply said, "Okay, Mama."

Once she'd left my room, I started to cry. I lay on the bed and buried my face in my pillow so no one would hear my sobs. I felt alone in this house with no one to comfort me, certainly not my mother, who seemed incapable of love and sympathy. Sometimes, she even scolded me or yelled at me when she heard me crying.

I didn't eat anything that day and had a bad week with more fights and disagreements with my mother. I decided that if I couldn't go to the boarding school, I should at least get to visit my cousins to lift my spirits. But I didn't have any money to buy bus tickets to visit them. I approached my mother and asked for money for the bus tickets, trying to sound sweet and pleasant.

She yelled at me instantly. "Are you a whore?" she cried. "Why do you always want to leave the house and visit people? Why don't you stay home? Only whores go outside the house."

"It's day," I insisted, "not night. I want to go out during the day."

"Day or night, it doesn't matter," she scoffed and stared me down. She refused to give me money for the bus tickets, no matter how much I begged and quarrelled about it.

Eventually, I started at the new high school called Wadijir, which means common school. It turned out to be a good school with both rich and poor students. Sara was attending a different high school, so I lost touch with her. I was anxious to make new friends but that was difficult when my mother wouldn't allow me to do much, so I was often bored and restless. We'd been living at the new place for three months when I finally met two kids from next door, Fardowsa and her brother Hussein, who were roughly my age and lived with their wealthy uncle. Both went to Wadijir, so we walked together to and from school, and since these children were our neighbors, my mother didn't object when I spent time with them. Fardowsa and Hussen shared one trait in common with Sara: wealth. Fardowsa's and Hussen's uncle had a lot of money and no one to spend it on. He had never been married and did not have a girlfriend. My mother told me once that many women would like to marry him because of his wealth, but he quickly rejected all of them. He lived privately and kept to himself. He might have preferred men to women, but no one talked about this directly.

As a result of all this, he spoiled Fardowsa and she got everything she wanted, including her own Mercedes with her own driver, just like Sara had. Hussen, on the other hand, was just a normal boy and did not receive the same attention from his uncle that Fardowsa did.

School itself was a challenge, since I wasn't very diligent about homework and so didn't get high marks, which displeased my mother. I was embarrassed when the school hung up the names of all the students and what grades they'd received. I had to learn Arabic and Latin at this school and was not very good at either language. Despite my average grades, my dream was to one day become a doctor or nurse. I worked as a volunteer for the Red Cross for two years while finishing high school. I liked helping people, and there were many people who needed help, including washing out the bloody wounds of men who had been injured in the civil war skirmishes outside of Mogadishu. I helped bandage them up and learned to endure the sound of their shouts and screams as they were overwhelmed with pain. It was impossible to help everyone because there was not enough staff, and medicine was sometimes limited.

I worked at two different hospitals. Dr. Mohmed, a friend of Rush's, worked at one of them. Dr. Mohmed had been educated in Italy and often visited our home. One night he even stayed overnight. The first day I ran across Dr. Mohmed at the hospital, he stopped me in the hall and asked why I was there, since he could see I was wearing a white smock. When I told him I was volunteering, he nodded appreciatively and smiled.

One day Dr. Mohmed told me he'd like to teach me the names of the different kinds of medicines—antibiotics, primcillin, malaria pills. Then when he was prescribing medications, it was my job to go to the hospital pharmacy and pick up the correct medication. This was an easy way to learn something about hospital work, and because I was interested in this, I learned quickly and became quite good at my job. This was the kind of job I dreamed about having in the future.

New Year's Eve, 1990

I planned to ring in the New Year with Sara and some friends who lived in northern Mogadishu. Despite our differences since Sara had moved to the wealthy side of town, we'd stayed in touch and arranged to get together every now and then. Sara and I and the others had made plans for this evening several months in advance. I'd bought some beautiful blue fabric out of which the tailor had sewn a dress. This had been expensive, but I was pleased with the result; the dress had shoulder pads and was tight around the waist and wider at the bottom.

Before Diina went out on her date with a smart snobbish boy, I asked if I could borrow her gold necklace for the night since she wasn't going to wear it. "No, you may not," she said and gave me a haughty look. "I don't want anything to happen to it."

I didn't want to beg for the necklace, so I said nothing more. I knew she was leaving on her date before me and that she would return after me, so I could just wear the necklace anyway and put it back before she got home. I had done this sort of thing before. Diina was selfish with her clothes and jewelry and never wanted to let me borrow anything, so I'd learned to help myself since she wasn't at home much anymore and I could return what I'd borrowed without her ever knowing.

In late afternoon of December 31, my mother and I were alone in the house. My brothers and Diina had already left to celebrate with their friends. Suddenly, there was a long banging and then explosions outside. My mother and I hurried to a window to peer outside.

"You're not going anywhere," my mother told me with an anxious frown. "It's not safe."

"Why not?" I sulked. "It's just fireworks."

My mother wasn't convinced, so I phoned Sara to see if she knew what was happening. "Yes, I heard the explosions, but I don't know what they were," she said.

Despite the explosions, Sara and I agreed to go ahead with our New Year's Eve plans. We'd meet in front of a theatre in northern Mogadishu where Halima Magool, a popular Somali singer, was giving a concert. After the concert, we would meet up with another one of my girlfriends and have dinner, then we'd go somewhere to drink Coca Cola and watch people celebrate the New Year. I slipped into my new blue dress, put Diina's gold necklace around my neck, and finished putting on my makeup. I had to meet Sara in front of the theatre at seven, so I was in a hurry to catch the bus. I didn't care if my mother had told me I couldn't go. I was nineteen and an adult now, and she could no longer dictate to me.

Before I had a chance to leave the house, the loud bangs and explosions started up again. They lasted longer than the previous ones, probably for more than ten minutes. I started to feel anxious, the way I had in Garbaharey many years ago when the city had been bombed. Finally, the bangs stopped again. My mother was in her bedroom, so I stepped quietly out of the house and into the street to see how people were reacting. I was met by a strange silence. Very few people had come out of their houses, and the ones that had looked as confused as I was. I dared myself to keep walking to the main street, where normally there was a lot of traffic and noisy, honking cars. Again, an eerie silence hung in the air. A single car passed by at full speed and didn't stop.

I hurried home, a knot in my throat, the silence pressing down around me. "Mama, I think something's wrong," I said when I was back inside the house.

My mother came out of her bedroom and looked more worried now than she had before. She turned on our small radio. A man's stern voice warned everyone to stay inside their homes and not to venture out. "What's going on?" she asked and looked at me nervously. "It's dangerous for a young girl like you to go out and take a bus to another neighborhood on New Year's Eve. Didn't you hear what the man on the radio said? We should stay home. I won't allow you to go out tonight!"

Despite the mysteriousness of what was happening and my mother's warnings, I still wanted to go to the concert and then party with my friends. I hadn't seen many of them for months since we'd graduated last summer. I called Sara again and asked if she knew anything more.

"Haven't you heard?" she asked excitedly. "War has broken out here in Mogadishu!"

"What?" I felt cold fear clamp down on my heart. "With whom?"

"I don't know. Listen to the news."

After Sara and I hung up, I told my mother what Sara had told me. "Call your Uncle Hassan," my mother said, her back stiffening. "Maybe he'll know."

Uncle Hassan was an army commander and worked for the government. I did as my mother asked and talked to Hassan's wife. She said that a civil war had broken out in the city, and it was best to travel away from Mogadishu. "We're packing up our things right now," she said. "Tell your mother you should do the same thing."

"Mama, they're leaving Mogadishu," I told her after I'd hung up. "She said we should leave too."

"We can't leave without your brothers and sisters." My mother took the phone receiver from me and started calling around to the rest of our family and friends. She received confirmation of the news: war had broken out to the north, but the road to Kismayo in southern Somalia was still open. This was the road people were taking to escape.

Since we lived near the harbor, there was a heavy population of foreigners in our neighborhood who had boats and made their living off fishing or helping to unload imported goods like gold, clothes, and building material that came into port. One of our neighbors from the Philippines came over to ask us some questions. Her name was Jing, and she was a tiny and thin woman with dusky red hair who had moved to Mogadishu with her husband when she'd gotten a guest worker job at an Arab embassy. Instantly, I could see how scared Jing was.

"What is happening?" she asked us, alarmed. "Why has a war started? Are you leaving the city?"

We told her we still didn't know. I'd never thought war would break out in Mogadishu, the capital city, because it was normally in the border areas where unrest and violent skirmishes erupted. "But if we end up leaving the city, you should come with us," I said.

Jing shook her head and wrung her hands together. "I want to stay here," she said. "I have a good job. I don't want to ruin that."

My mother and I tried to comfort her, but she soon turned around and left, just as frightened and confused as when she'd come.

At 7:00 pm, the radio announcer said that all New Year's activities had been cancelled due to the outbreak of war. They told us everyone should stay home and lock their doors. That was the last thing they said on the radio before the airwaves went out.

Mogadishu Transformed

My mother and I, alone in the house, waited for my brothers and Diina to return. We waited all night, and when it was morning, they still hadn't come home. The house felt strange without them, empty and silent. We were a big family, and I was used to noise and raised voices. When my brothers and sister were present, I often retreated to my bedroom for privacy, but now that they were gone and my mother and I didn't know where they were, I missed them. We constantly wondered if something had happened to them. As the hours passed and turned into another day and they still hadn't returned, our fears mounted and became unbearable.

When Diina and my brothers had not returned home after two days, my mother called Uncle Hassan to see if he could help. My uncle told us what he knew: they were alive, but the government had taken them to a place where they would learn how to shoot to prepare them to take part in the fight against the Hawiye clan. The Hawiye clan was the largest clan in Somalia, located primarily in southern and central Somalia although they had influential subdivisions that were dominant in Mogadishu. In short, the military, with orders from the government, had seized them along with our cousins and many others, to train them and build a Somalian army to fight in the war.

"But they are children!" my mother cried. "Diina's a girl!"

When she told me what my uncle had just said, we both burst into tears. But Uncle Hassan claimed the government had made the decision and there was nothing any of us could do about it.

Now I was scared. I tried to picture Diina and my brothers in military uniforms with guns in their hands, patrolling the violent streets. How could we save them? How could we all get out of town? My mother, however, now that she knew what we were up against, had turned calm and collected. "We can't leave," she told me. "We have to stay here. Maybe they'll come back at some point. If we aren't here, how will they find us?"

Beneath my mother's external calm, though, I sensed traces of anxiety, frustration, and anger. "They're children!" she said repeatedly. "They cannot fight against other clans. Don't they see they're just *children*?"

Every time she said those words, I felt a stab in my heart. I knew nothing about clans. I'd been raised in Mogadishu and therefore spoke the dialect of the capital city. In my eyes, all Somalians had the same language, color, culture, tradition, and religion, and I had a hard time seeing the other clans as my enemies since we'd lived side by side up until now. All foreigners were advised to leave the country, and after a few days Jing came over to say goodbye. On the first day of the war Jing had been hesitant to leave because of her job, but now she seemed happy and relieved for the opportunity to leave Somalia.

Despite that many people were fleeing Mogadishu, my mother continued to refuse to leave without all her children, and I didn't want to leave my old mother alone in the middle of a civil war. My mother was stubborn and in denial about certain things. She insisted that we didn't have to flee because we were women, and she believed it was only the men from the Darod clan that the Hawiye clan were after. But we were still afraid of getting hit by a random bullet out in the streets, so we stayed home most of the time.

One day when the weather was quite hot, I heard the neighbors across the street start yelling and screaming. I hurried over to see what was happening and discovered that the family's father had been taken prisoner by several members of the Hawiye clan. Out on the road, a large container of water had been placed over a bonfire that kept the water boiling. He was to be thrown alive into the boiling water. The accused man, wearing ragged and clumsy work clothes, stood hunched and quite still, like someone who had given up a long time ago.

I couldn't believe these men from the Hawiye clan, no matter how angry and determined, intended to boil a man alive out in the street in front of his wife and children. The accused man had four children between the ages of ten and seventeen. I had played with them often. The eldest daughter begged the men to spare her father's life. The smaller children cried, and a couple of them dropped to their knees and started to pray.

"Be quiet or you'll be next!" one of the men from the Hawiye clan shouted at the accused man's family. He pointed his gun at them to emphasize his words. "He works for Barre."

All I knew was that my neighbor was well-liked throughout the neighborhood and had worked as a police officer for twenty years. He'd always been helpful and sweet-tempered. I cried along with the family, although I stood far enough away from them for safety reasons.

Several neighbors hurried out of their homes, shocked and angry. "He's a good man!" they cried while also keeping their distance. "Why are you doing this?"

The Hawiye men started shouting back at the protesting neighbors. The sun beat down on my head and I started to sweat. I stared at the bubbling water in the pot over the fire, and then back at my defeated neighbor. My whole body shook. The man's wife and eldest daughter turned away and threw up. Finally, I couldn't stand to watch any longer and ran back into the house with my mother. I heard the screams and cries from my neighbors as the accused man was boiled alive. I was so frightened I didn't leave the house for three days. I'd learned a painful truth: there was such extreme injustice in the world that a man could be tortured and executed in the most painful way imaginable without any evidence of his guilt.

The chaos of that day was just an example of what was happening throughout the city. Farmers, the unemployed, and criminals had suddenly taken power in Mogadishu. All of them had been hit the hardest by the high unemployment in Barre's government, and they were starving and desperate. But if they committed a crime, they would receive harsh punishment, including severe beatings in prison, so they took the extreme step of overthrowing the government. It was jarring and strange to see so many people in a mass exodus, hastily packing up a few possessions and then escaping the city. Members of the Hawiye clan started moving into the abandoned houses, taking possession of any money, gold, clothes, and cars that had been left behind. My mother and I tried to ignore the chaos happening outside our front door, and every day prayed for the safe return of my brothers and Diina.

But soon my mother and I had nearly run out of food. We only had left a little canned tuna, peeled tomatoes, and rice, so one day I set my fears aside and headed out to find someone who was selling food. The streets were eerily empty and quiet, like a ghost town. I wandered into the main area of town where the shops were, but nothing was open. Everything was deserted.

Then I ran across a girl who was about ten years old and crying on a street corner. Her clothes were soaked with blood, and her face was also bloody from where someone had beaten her. Horrified, I looked around to see if anyone were around to help, but no one was.

Finally, I went up to the sobbing child and asked, "What's the matter? What happened? Where are your parents?"

The girl clutched at her torn clothing and told me that five men had raped her. "Hurry and get away," she told me. "The men are nearby!"

I felt my head turn light, dizzy with fear. "What about you?" I asked.

"I can't get up. I don't think I will survive." The girl started to cry again. "It's dangerous for you. Run! Run!"

"Please, tell me where you live," I said.

"I'm homeless." She told me she was a street child and had no parents or anyone to help her. "Go!" she said again. "Run!"

My body was trembling, and my stomach in such knots that I felt sick. I bent over in the street and vomited, and then hurried away from the girl. There was nothing I could do for her. I forgot about food and started back toward home. No one dared to conduct normal business when a war was going on.

I walked down narrow side streets because I didn't dare walk on the main street where all the cars were driving extra fast to avoid the gunfire. I kept thinking about the homeless girl who had been raped. If only I'd been able to help her. As I approached my house, I ran across several soldiers sitting alongside the road, all armed with guns. One of them spotted me and said, "Where are you going, darling?"

I wondered why he'd called me "darling" because it was not a word a strange man used to speak to a girl he didn't know. But these men were in uniform, military men, so I assumed I could trust them.

"Do you know any stores that are open?" I asked. "I need to buy food."

"No. No I don't." He stood up and smiled in a way that made me uncomfortable. He walked toward me. When I saw the other soldiers laughing behind him, I grew frightened. Something was wrong. *Five men*, I thought. *There are five men.*

I started to back up as the man continued to move forward. "Are you alone?" he asked me with that same nasty smile on his face.

"No!" I shouted. "I'm with my father and brother!"

The man looked startled and glanced around. The others grabbed their guns and jumped to their feet. My heart pounded and I broke into a sweat, and not just because it was noon, and not because the sun was burning down on my scalp. I turned on my heel and began running away as fast as I could.

Behind me, I heard the men curse and then shout to each other, "She is alone! After her, after her!"

I never ran so hard in my life. I knew that if they caught me, they would rape me. These were Hawiye soldiers, and I was sure they were the ones who had raped the little girl. As I ran, I glanced over my shoulder. Two of the men continued to chase me. "Papa, Rush, help me!" I cried, still pretending that my father and brother were nearby.

I veered onto the main road where there would likely be more people around. I was no longer afraid of the fast traffic. The two soldiers stopped chasing me. "You little whore!" they shouted. "You're very lucky!"

Finally, I stopped running and stayed on the main road for as long as I could before I snuck back home. I was breathing hard, and my damp clothes stuck to my back. Ugly things were happening that I'd never experienced before. Doing a simple task like going out to find food meant I risked getting raped.

My mother and I soon realized the time where we could safely leave Mogadishu had passed. We had stayed too long and now we were trapped. There was no food and nowhere to buy any. And shooting had broken out everywhere in our district, so stepping outside into the street was no longer safe. We hid in our house, listened to all the fighting outside, and prayed for a way out of this mess.

One day, my mother and I heard a jarring rumble from down the street. We ran to look out the window and saw a military tank pull up in front of our house, followed by several cars. Uncle Hassan stepped out of one of the cars in his military uniform along with several soldiers, all who were armed. Uncle Hassan came to the door with a stern expression on his face.

"You have to hurry," he said. "This area is dangerous. You need to leave. I don't have enough soldiers if shooting starts."

My mother and I didn't have time to get our passports or any other documentation. We didn't pack any clothes.

We simply ran out of the house in our bare feet and jumped into the tank.

I took one last look at our house, aware even then it was probably the last time I would see it. Several of my neighbors stood outside, staring at us as if they'd never seen us before. I bowed my head and couldn't look at them. I felt we were cowards for fleeing so abruptly, and in a military tank my uncle had sent especially for us.

Space was cramped inside the tank. To keep from feeling too claustrophobic, I glanced up at the small window at the top of the tank. I could see a wedge of the grey and cloudy sky, although it wasn't the season for rain. Then I realized I was seeing smoke. The city was on fire and there was smoke and red, flaming embers in the air.

"This is the safest vehicle in war," my uncle said as the tank rumbled down the road. "It's protected from ordinary bullets. If someone shoots missiles or bombs at us, we could burn, but otherwise we're safe in here."

I wasn't sure if I felt comforted by this or not.

The roads were empty, although we could hear many sounds from every direction—explosions and the snap of gunfire. Uncle Hassan told my mother and me that he was taking us to the Afsiyoone airport on the outskirts of Mogadishu. As we got closer to the airport, someone started shooting at the tank. The shots were fired from the houses near the road as we passed by. The tank picked up speed while some of Uncle Hassan's soldiers fired back. I put my hands to my ears and tried to block the sound out.

"Why are they shooting at us?" my mother asked, worried.

"The tank," my uncle said. "They can see it's a tank from Barre's government." He explained that the Darod clan was in power right now because of President Barre, but the Hawiye clan was hellbent on overthrowing the government, and so all members of the Darod clan were forced to flee for their own safety. "Many Somalians are on the run right now," Uncle Hassan added. "Many have been killed trying to get away."

Finally, we made it past the bullets and entered the airport area, which was like a small town. There was an international airport and field hospital in the "new airport," and a military base located in the "old airport." The old airport was used to train military pilots and there was also an education building. Both inside and outside the old airport were "villas" that housed government and military personnel and their families. Many people who had fled Mogadishu also came here to live until they could figure out where to go next. The old airport had become a makeshift refugee camp.

My uncle brought my mother and me to a villa in the old airport where a military pilot, who had recently fled the city, had been living. Here we would stay, temporarily, and use its kitchen, toilet, and one of the bedrooms that wasn't used for storage. There was no light or water in the villa, but Uncle Hassan gave us a jerry can containing thirty liters of petroleum which we could use for cooking and oil lamps. As for water, we along with everyone else living at the airport had to fetch water from a distant well.

After we were safely at the villa, Uncle Hassan told us he was leaving us here. "I need to escape town and help fight the war," he said. My mother and I were terrified of being left alone in the airport during the middle of a civil war and asked him not to go, but Uncle Hassan was firm that this was necessary. I couldn't help but feel that Uncle Hassan was abandoning us and leaving us behind to save his own life.

My mother and I had to quickly adapt to life in our new surroundings. One of our most pressing needs was water. During the day it was difficult to get to the well because all the other refugees were going there too, which caused long lines and hours of waiting. My mother and I agreed that I should fetch water in the evening when most people had gone to bed. Often, I would bring some water back to families with children, since I knew it was harder for those families to get to the well.

Still, most of our neighbors who lived in nearby villas kept to themselves. My mother knew a couple of the neighbors and talked to them, but otherwise we were just as isolated as everyone else. People were largely quiet and insecure. Because there was so much clan warfare in Somalia and the civil war was between clans, we didn't know who in the camp of refugees were friendly and peaceful and who were enemies. The population was constantly in flux, with new people moving in every day and people leaving just as suddenly as they'd arrived. A lot of us spent most of our time sitting in our houses and waiting for the war to end. I noticed a change in my mother's mood. She stopped shouting so much and became sad, lonely, and quiet, often sleeping or staring off into space with a dazed look in her eyes.

To help fight off my boredom and apprehension while also giving myself something useful to do, I started working at the field hospital located at the airport. Many women and children had been shot on their way to the airport. Two doctors and four nurses worked at the field hospital, which was not enough medical staff to care for all the wounded, so I was allowed to help them because of my First Aid background and my work with the Red

Cross. I administered injections, washed wounds, fetched food and water. I helped with births and surgeries and picked up medication and bandages for the doctors. At first, I couldn't bear to see so many wounded and helpless people, but eventually I grew accustomed to it. I worked tirelessly and received praise every day from the doctors and nurses that I was doing a good job.

My mother and I had been at the airport for a few days when the war spread from Mogadishu and into Afsiyoone. Military troops and tanks invaded the city. Gunfire became more commonplace. I told my mother it was probably best if we left Mogadishu altogether. "It's not safe here," I told her.

But when my mother talked to the soldier who was patrolling the encampment to make sure everyone was okay, he said the war would probably stop after a few days because the Hawiye clan were apparently losing and would soon retreat. My mother believed the soldier and said we should stay put.

I wasn't sure I shared the soldier's opinion. I could hear that the shooting was getting closer. "Mama, he's probably not telling the truth," I said after the soldier had moved on. "You can see there are more wounded people coming to the field hospital." I took a deep breath and then added, "I want to leave. Now."

My mother cast her eyes down and wouldn't look me in the eye. "Then you'll have to travel alone," she said and looked both sorry and annoyed. "I won't be coming with you."

"Mama!" I was startled and hurt that she'd even suggest we should separate.

"I can probably find someone who's going to Baardheere who can take you along so you can stay with your aunt," she said.

I shook my head. I couldn't imagine traveling without her, but she refused to leave Mogadishu. She was still clinging to the hope she could return to our house and wait for my brothers and Diina to show up.

I continued to stay at the military pilot's villa with my mother even though I was unhappy about it. I was often alone because my mother went to talk to one of the neighbors. They were probably talking about the war. I was lonely without my friends and brothers and even Diina to talk to. The villa felt quiet and empty without my brothers' teasing and without Diina bursting into a room without knocking or arguing with someone nearby. I also wondered what Sara was doing and hoped that she and her family were okay. Had they escaped Mogadishu? I had no way of knowing.

With so much alone time and nothing to do, I couldn't keep my mind from wandering down a dark path. What if I died in the war before I saw my brothers and Diina and all my relatives again? Even though I was nineteen years old, I still worried about whether I would go to hell after I died. These were the same thoughts that had plagued me almost a decade ago when I'd hidden under my aunt's bed during the bombing in Garbaharey. I reminded myself I hadn't committed any of the major sins—I was still a virgin and hadn't stolen or killed anyone. But I wasn't sure if that was enough to warrant entry into heaven. Now that I was older, I analyzed things more and started to question much of what I was told. I still doubted that the war was going to end soon. I'd already seen and experienced so much that was horrible—our neighbor boiled to death, the child who had been raped by the soldiers, the soldiers chasing me down the street to rape me. I was afraid all this chaos and horror would drag on rather than end abruptly.

The Funeral

The war continued for another two weeks. Now the whole city was without electricity, which meant our refrigerator was not working. Food was becoming scarce again. One day I ate cold spaghetti with a sour smell because there was nothing else to eat. Occasionally, a couple of my cousins would stop by with spaghetti and a few cans of tomato and tuna that they'd stolen at the container port. These stolen items helped feed my mother and me for a couple more days, but then that food also ran out.

One afternoon, I grew desperate for food and started walking up the main street near the airport. I came across a family of seven who were gathered around a man, the father, lying in the street. The man was shouting and crying out in pain. A woman and some children were gathered around him, trying to hold him down and care for him.

I hurried over. "What happened?" I asked the adult woman who I assumed was the injured man's wife.

"We were just trying to leave town," the woman sobbed. "Someone shot him!"

The woman and children pointed to the window of a house across the street. The woman had no idea why someone was shooting at them. They were poor and had nothing with them except for their clothes. The injured man was a factory worker, about forty years old and very thin. He'd been shot in the middle of his left thigh and was moaning incoherently. Blood was streaming out of his wound. I thought maybe I could help, since I worked at the field hospital. I kneeled next to the man, forgetting that I was now in danger myself. I had no idea whether there were still hoodlums up in the window shooting at people. The woman and I tried to bandage the man with several layers of cloth. She handed me her scarf and I tied that around the man's leg. We also used my garbasaar, and the woman took off her own blouse and asked a couple of her children to remove their shirts so I could use them as bandages. But the blood kept running like an open faucet.

I looked around frantically, wondering if I could run back to the field hospital and get someone to come to him. But there wasn't time. The man's moaning grew fainter, and finally he simply died. His family started to sob again. The oldest daughter, a teenager, did not cry, just stood speechless with her hand over her mouth. The smaller children cried and circled their father's body, and the youngest clung to her mother's dress. I hadn't been so close to a man when he'd died since I'd witnessed the execution many years ago. I stood up and backed away from the grieving family. I couldn't help but think this was only the beginning.

The blood continued to gush from the man's thigh. I stared down at him and his stricken wife and started to question whether he was dead, after all. "Maybe he's just unconscious," I said.

But his wife fiercely shook her head. "No," she said. "He is dead, and I do not know where to bury him."

The oldest daughter bent over and started to dry heave. The other children continued to cry. Two of the children were sitting on the ground and crying, while two other children were standing and holding hands. "I live right over there," I said. "Come with me. We'll help you bury him."

Despite that the dead man was thin, he was still heavy. I took hold of his legs while his wife took hold of the man's head. The two oldest children picked up one of his arms while the youngest children followed us. Together, we started the long process of carrying him to the airport. Walking about a mile while carrying a heavy body was difficult and challenging, especially because the weather was so hot. We had to set the man's body down several times along the way so we could rest and catch our breath before starting the whole process again. The blood continued to flow out of him and mix with my own sweat. The day was so hot and bright I was almost blinded by the sun. At one point, I didn't care whether I lived or died. I didn't care if there were snipers across the road, pointing a gun at me through a house window. I just continued to move forward with the dead man's body in my arms.

When we reached the military pilot's house, I shouted, "Mama, mama, come and help us!"

My mother hurried out the door, her hair askew and standing on end as if she'd just received an electrical shock. She looked confused because we'd interrupted her afternoon nap. "What?" she asked, and then, seeing the body of the dead man in our arms, she began to sob. "Help, help!" she cried.

Finally, a man walked over to us. He moved slowly and carefully, as if he knew he was entering a volatile situation and wasn't sure if he wanted to get involved. My mother knew this man slightly, so I told him the whole story of how the dead man had been shot. Now all we needed was to find a place to bury him. Since the pilot's house was state-owned, there was enough ground for us to dig a hole and give the man a decent burial.

"I'll get some men who can help us bury the body," the man said quietly and walked away.

The dead man's wife and I picked up the body again and placed it in shade under a tree.

My mother turned to me with sudden anger in her eyes. "What were you doing out on that dangerous street?" she asked.

I moved a few feet away so the dead man's wife and children could not hear my mother and I argue. The dead man's family were standing awkwardly over his body, uncertain what to do, their eyes sad and empty.

I reminded my mother that I'd gone out in search of food because we didn't have much left. Nevertheless, I asked her about giving the family a little something to eat and drink.

"We only have pasta and tea left," she said, frowning, "and we need to save something for tomorrow."

Still, when we looked over at the grieving family under the tree, doing nothing seemed cruel, so I invited them into the house.

Once inside, they sat on the floor and looked down silently. They probably felt they were a burden and an imposition. I glanced over at my mother, and she nodded grimly, and I quickly heated up some tea and pasta, although it was not normal to serve guests cooked pasta without any sauce, meat, or salad.

"We don't have any salt," I apologized to the wife.

"Would you like some sugar for the pasta instead?" my mother asked.

They all nodded. We set down before them a cup of tea, some sugar, and a kilo of pasta. They smiled gratefully and then grabbed at the food and the tea. They ate as if they hadn't eaten in days. The tea was gone almost immediately. I made another kilo of pasta and a new pitcher of tea, even though this severely cut down on the food supply my mother and I had left.

After they'd eaten, the family thanked us for the food. I noticed how the wife and the children smiled more and made eye contact with us. Yet I could also see how hungry they were and how hopeless their lives had become, and now things had been made even worse by the death of the father. Overcome with sadness and pity, I ran out of the house and started to cry. I sat down on the burning ground, overheated from the sun, and cried, "Allah, help us!" I looked first up at the heavens, at the bright and scorching sky, and then back down to earth. The dead man's body was not far away, and he looked as if he, too, was staring up at the sky and waiting for something. A few flies were buzzing around him and crawling over his face.

A few minutes passed before I had composed myself. I realized my blouse was soaked through with sweat. I climbed to my feet, brushed the tears from my face, and went back inside.

Three more hours passed. The man who'd promised he would find some men to help us bury the body had still not returned. My mother grew worried. Eventually, we had to face the stark reality: the man was not coming back. He'd walked away and abandoned us. My mother started knocking on nearby doors and shouting, "We need help! We need to bury a man."

After my mother had knocked on about ten house doors, we had rounded up eight volunteers to help, three men and five women. My mother called them all together and explained the situation. "We need to bury the man behind that tree," she said and pointed to a large tree that stood nearby. "We must give him a proper funeral. His wife and children are staying with us and are entitled to it."

The men rounded up shovels and picks and began digging the hole. Because it was so hot, I went inside, made cold drinks, and then offered them to the men. While the men were digging the hole, the women carried the dead man to the door of our house, where they washed his body, straightened his hair, and lowered his eyelids so he would look peaceful and serene. Then the women wrapped him in white sheets. My mother called his wife and children over and asked if they'd like to say goodbye to their beloved husband and father.

The wife, petrified, stared at his body wrapped in the sheets and didn't say a word. The two youngest children started to cry again and wanted to touch him to see if they could wake him up. My mother and I held the children back so they wouldn't interfere with the wife's goodbye. "Your father is at peace now," I told the children. "He's going to paradise, and you will see him again someday."

The dead man's family finished their goodbyes and wandered into our house. When the men had dug the grave hole several feet deep, they carried the dead body over and set him down inside. They stood around the makeshift tomb, and I could see they were praying to Allah to help the man and his bereaved family. Then they shovelled dirt over the grave and it was finished. The dead man had been buried.

Suddenly, the dead man's wife began to scream from inside the house, as if it only dawned on her now that her husband was dead. She ran outside, yanking at big tufts of her hair, and then back inside. The children stood at the door, even the older ones, and began to cry when they saw their mother in such despair. I hurried into the house, led the grief-stricken family into my room, and closed the door so they could have privacy in their grief.

My mother and I thanked the people who had helped us and then returned inside the house to help the dead man's family. The man's wife was still crying. "I don't know where to go," the woman sobbed and wiped her eyes with the sleeve of her blouse.

The woman's dialect was so thick that my mother had difficulty understanding her, so I helped translate whatever my mother couldn't understand. "We have no money," the woman continued. "Where can we go without money?"

"Do you have any other family?" I asked the woman.

The woman nodded but explained her family lived on the Kenya-Somalia border, about 617 miles, and Mogadishu til Geedo 548 miles.

I translated to my mother what the woman had said. "You can stay with us here until you can get a lift somewhere," my mother said. "But we don't have enough food for everyone tomorrow."

I was upset by how harsh and dismissive my mother sounded. Despite this family's unbearable loss, my mother was neither helpful nor hospitable. She was making it clear that she wanted the family to move out as quickly as possible.

The family stayed with us for two days. We ran out of food so my mother went to the neighbors and asked if they could spare anything. We got sugar and rice from the neighbors to help tide us over. All the while my mother also asked around to see if anyone was going to Kenya.

Eventually, a family came to us and said they could drive the dead man's wife and children to a town a hundred miles away. This was wonderful news because it would get the dead man's family closer to the Kenya border. My mother gave the dead man's wife a little money and a pound of sugar.

Once the family left, I never saw them again, but to this day I can picture their faces— tired, hungry, scared, desperate, on the edge between living and dying. I still wonder if that family survived the war, but there's no way for me to know.

After the experience with the dead man, I promised myself that I wouldn't go out shopping anymore. It simply wasn't worth the risk. Now when I wasn't volunteering at Lazaret Hospital, I stayed inside the house with my mother. I helped her with housekeeping, and I slept and daydreamed about returning home and resuming my past life. Occasionally, we could hear gunfire or explosions in the distance.

But the house was hot and stuffy, and I soon became bored again with only my mother for company. My promise to myself that I would stay home gradually drifted away. One day I decided to check if Aunt Halimo was still alive. She had a close relationship with one of my cousins whose parents had died. When my cousin's husband died a few years ago, Aunt Halimo closed her clothing store in Garbaharey to come live with my cousin in Mogadishu.

In Somalia, it's common for relatives to take care of other family members' children. But now my aunt was living alone in my cousin's house because the rest of the family had fled Mogadishu several weeks ago when the fighting began. My aunt had chosen to stay behind and look after the house until the trouble had passed. Now she was alone, and the fighting had escalated, so I was worried about her and wanted to make sure she was alright.

My mother insisted that I shouldn't go off alone to check on my aunt. "It's dangerous," she reminded me, and I could see in her face how upset she was.

I knew my mother was right about the danger. Aunt Halimo lived seven miles away, and that was a long distance to walk on my own when a war was going on. But as scared as I was, I also felt it was my duty, and I couldn't just sit in the house all day for weeks with nothing to do. At night, I dreamed of Somali men chasing me and shooting at me, trying to kill me.

I said goodbye to my mother despite her protests. Once she grabbed my hand and ordered me to stay inside, but I just pulled away and told her I'd be back soon. Before I left, I decided I needed a little food to take with me. A neighbor didn't have much to spare but did loan me a pound of sugar and a package of tea. Happy and full of confidence, I headed toward the Shiirkole neighborhood in northern Mogadishu.

I followed the wide main street which used to be filled with noisy cars and people going to the cafés and the cinema, but today there was only paper blowing back and forth in the otherwise empty street. I grew less confident the further away I walked. I was always glancing over my shoulder to make sure no one was coming up from behind me, and I constantly checked all the side streets to keep track of where I was. A single car passed by. I shuddered inside and felt the situation resembled the day we all feared most: Judgment Day. I simply didn't know who was in the car and what the man might do. Some young men shot at people for fun, for no reason, like the guys who'd shot the factory worker.

After I had walked over two miles, I saw a lot of blood on the street, fresh blood. My head spun and the world turned black before my eyes. When I recovered, I thought about turning around and going back, but I was so close to my aunt now. I decided to risk the danger and continue. I walked gingerly down the street, past puddles of blood that glittered in the sunlight. How strange it was that there were no people around. It was like there had been a nuclear holocaust and I was the only survivor walking the barren streets.

Eventually, I came to an area where the university was located. A group of three young men hurried out of one of the campus buildings and rushed over to me. At first, I flinched when I saw them, but I quickly could tell they were students and were also scared and would not harm me.

"Where are you going?" one of the students asked. He was about 25 years old, a little overweight, and very much a city person. I could hear it in the way he spoke Mogadishu very carefully and delicately.

"I'm going to the Shiirkole quarter," I told the students, relieved to see friendly faces.

"You shouldn't do that," he said. "It's dangerous to walk alone here. You should go back."

"I can't. I have to make sure my aunt is okay."

Just then, gunfire erupted around us. We threw ourselves down to the ground. The shooting continued for about ten minutes. We didn't know who was shooting at us or why. "We are students!" one of the students shouted. "What do you want?"

Ten young armed men came running towards us. It was impossible to tell what clan they were from. "Hurry!" they yelled. "Get away from here!"

The students and I leapt to our feet and started running. I ran in a different direction than they did because I was still determined to get to my aunt's place. I ran as fast and as hard as I could, my lungs working overtime, until I was in a different area where there was no longer any gunfire. I slowed down a little but continued to jog until I reached my cousin's house.

But when I knocked on the door, no one answered. Confused, I wondered what would happen if my aunt had fled, after all, and I had to return all the way back to the airport. "Hello, it's me, Abdia!" I shouted, for Abdia was my nickname. "Are you home, Auntie?"

The door swung open, and my aunt stepped out, tears rolling down her cheeks. "Abdia," she said.

We held each other and cried in relief. "What are you doing here?" she asked. "Is your family still here? Has someone died?"

"It's just my mother and me living at the airport." I paused and then explained how Diina and my brothers had been forcibly taken to fight in the war.

"How horrible," Aunt Halimo said. "Come in."

The apartment was small and not well furnished. Aunt Halimo told me she didn't have enough food and had no idea when the grocery stores would reopen. Almost everyone from the neighborhood had fled and she was very isolated. Now she wanted to leave Mogadishu, but she didn't have a car and had no means to get out of town. I gave her the sugar and tea I'd brought along, which was a relief to my aunt because she also had nothing to drink.

After my aunt made tea, we sat down on the sofa to chat. Suddenly, there was a knock on the door. We glanced at each other in dread and didn't say a word. For all we knew, there were robbers at the door, though I didn't know if robbers would bother to knock first. Finally, I snuck into the hallway and looked through the small peephole in the door. It was my aunt's neighbor, Sagal, a woman she had known for many years.

When I opened the door, Segal stepped inside. She looked at me and then at my aunt. "God, are you still here?" she said to Aunt Halimo. "You haven't left yet?"

Aunt Halimo shook her head. "I'm all alone," she said. "Thieves come out at night. I've heard them robbing the other apartments."

Segal explained that she, her husband, and their children had just returned home to pick up their refrigerator and then they were going to leave again immediately. "You can come with us if you'd like," she said. "You will have to pack fast."

"Yes, thank you!" my aunt said, then looked questioningly at me.

"No, I can't go with you," I told her. "I have to go back to Mama."

I couldn't stay to help Aunt Halimo pack because it was already getting dark. My aunt and I said goodbye and then I started back with a happy and clear conscience, knowing that she was okay and was getting the chance to leave Mogadishu.

I was almost home when I heard gunfire in the distance. It was completely dark now and I didn't dare walk on the main street, so I ran along small roads and carefully watched everything behind and in front of me. Fortunately, no one was around that I could see.

My mother was sitting on a chair in front of the house when I returned. "There you are," she said impatiently and crossed her arms, although I could also see the relief on her face. "Why are you coming home so late? I told you it's dangerous out there."

"I saw Aunt Halimo," I told her.

But my mother's mind was elsewhere, and she didn't sound happy with my news. "You must never do that again," she said sadly. "There was a violent attack near here. Many people have been killed."

I told her Aunt Halimo was leaving the city with her neighbors. "We should leave to," I said. "We can't wait any longer. Like you said, it's dangerous."

But my mother shook her head. "I don't think the war will last that much longer," she said vaguely.

I exhaled in frustration. My mother did not know what was truly going on in the city. She stayed home all day and had shut out the real world of war and mayhem, while I'd been out in the streets and experienced the chaos first-hand. But I still didn't feel like I could leave her.

In a strange way, I got used to feeling afraid. I accepted that Judgment Day must be coming because I had read the Qur'an which pointed out several signs you can recognize that indicate the end of times. People will kill each other until, finally, the heavens will roar, and the remaining people on earth will die in a sweeping flood. All the killing and violent death I'd seen so far suggested the Qur'an's prophecy was beginning to come true.

I wondered every day when Allah would come and help us out of the chaos that Somalia had become. Death and the afterlife were constantly on my mind. Otherwise, I was not especially religious. It was hard to stay religious when the country was falling apart. Most people were confused and powerless. They didn't know what they should do to protect themselves. Survival required people to think differently than they normally did. Many people had lost their families and everything they owned—houses, money, property—and did not expect to live the leisurely life they once had. All refugees were equal now. Most people had abandoned the belief that Somalia would ever become a peaceful place again.

I didn't mention to my mother the horrors I'd experienced while going to visit my aunt. Instead, I went to bed and stayed there for three days.

One evening when I was working at the hospice of the field hospital, President Siyaad Barre himself arrived in a tank. He and his two sons stepped out of the tank and walked into the sick bay to greet us. Barre was a small wrinkled old man, and as he spoke, a man held a lamp to his face so we could see him. *Wow,* I thought, surprised that he'd come to visit us in this way. But I also had a foreboding sense that Barre had come with bad news. His face looked sad and crushed.

I stood behind the doctors as Barre told us the war had advanced to just outside the airport and he needed to leave now. He had come to say goodbye and to warn us. "Everyone has to leave as soon as possible," he announced. "Take the wounded with you."

Then he and his two sons returned to their tank and drove off towards Kismayo. Pandemonium broke out after that. Doctors and nurses left their posts and their patients as they ran off to their houses or to their cars to drive away, following Barre. Some of the wounded rose out of their beds and fled as well. Unfortunately, there were many men who were too wounded to escape on their own, and they were mostly left behind as people ran to save their own lives. "Help us!" some of the wounded shouted. "Take us with you!"

But desperation had taken over, and Barre's request that we take the wounded with us was forgotten. We simply wanted to escape with our own lives. We could hear gunfire approaching the hospital and loud, menacing shouting. I ran with the rest of them, and as I left the hospital, I saw smoke rising over the city. I felt like the bottom had just dropped out of my life. Everything I knew and loved was gone and replaced by this chaos.

Mama, I thought. *I need to get back to Mama.*

My heart in my throat, I ran back home to our villa. "We have to leave *now!*" I yelled at my mother. "President Barre said so."

Finally, my mother's face registered the reality of the situation. "But we don't have a car," she said. "How will we get away?"

Still, we started packing our small bags with what few possessions we had left. There was a stern knock on the door. "You people in there!" a guard shouted. "Open up! You must run away now! The Hawiye clan is close to the airport. They're killing women, children, and old people."

My mother and I looked at each other in terror. "Maybe we should just stay here," she said. "It doesn't matter if Barre fled. We're women. No one will want to kill or rape us."

"What?" I was shocked by her reaction, which was naïve and passive. She misunderstood the situation and still seemed in denial of the danger we were facing. "You heard what the guard just said. The Hawiye clan are killing women and children."

I stuffed more clothes into our bags. Then I stepped outside and waved for my mother to come. She hesitated but then followed me outside.

Out on the street, people were hurrying past, some carrying bags and some not. When they saw us, they shouted, "They're coming! Run, run!"

Driven by the panic in their voices, my mother and I started running as well. All I could think was, *I knew it! I knew we should have escaped from Mogadishu long ago!*

When we were outside the airport area, we ran across a Toyota Land Cruiser that had been hit by an explosive. A man was lying inside, gravely wounded. "Help me, help me, take me with you!" he screamed.

The people in our group didn't look at the man or talk to him as they ran past. My mother and I paused and then hurried over to him, but the lower half of his body was wounded so badly, and he was bleeding so terribly, that there was nothing we could do for him. I felt like surrendering then and giving up on fleeing. What was the point if the Hawiye clan were just going to catch us and kill us anyway?

"Please take me with you," the man begged us.

My mother was touched by him, but she also saw there was no point. "We are sorry," she said. "We can't help you. We don't have a car. We're women and can't carry you."

We had to leave him. "Help, someone help, I beg you!" he cried again.

After we'd moved on, his cries suddenly stopped. I didn't know if he was no longer crying and begging because he'd accepted his fate or because he had died.

The Escape from Mogadishu

We were escaping the city with many families who knew each other. Eventually, we made it to the coast. A few cars were driving by along the coastal highway. Two or three cars pulled to the side of the road and shouted that they had room to take some of us.

My mother, three old women, and a few mothers with young children quickly climbed into the cars. Only there was no room left for me in any of them. "I don't want to leave my daughter!" my mother cried and tried to crawl back out of the car she was in. She'd thought I was behind her and, in the crying and chaos, didn't realize I hadn't climbed into a car because there was no more room.

"I'll be fine!" I shouted to her. "See you later."

I only said that to reassure my mother, and in the back of my mind I hoped that she would still push her way back out of the car so we wouldn't get separated. But my mother stopped fighting to get out. I was confused and frightened and not sure what to do.

Three women who had also climbed into the cars yelled for two young men, Kamaal and Josef, to take care of their sisters. "Take care of my daughter too!" my mother shouted.

Then the cars drove off. I watched the cars disappear in the distance. My mother had left me! I felt abandoned and empty inside.

Because my mother had asked Kamaal and Josef to look after me, I turned helplessly to them and their two overweight younger sisters. I knew they were all from the Darod clan. I didn't know Kamaal or his brothers or sisters very well, but I had no choice but to put my faith in them now. This was the new group I had to travel with. Kamaal was 26 and the oldest of the family, a history and law student at the University of Mogadishu. He was clean-shaven, handsome, talkative, and seemed a very grown man. It was clear from the start that he would become the leader of our group. His brother Josef, an engineering student, had a beard and a shaven head. He was shorter than Kamaal, and like his sisters was overweight. He was quieter and more reserved than any of us. He showed little interest in talking to the other members of our group. He had cigarettes with him and liked to smoke a lot.

"Come on," Kamaal finally said, and we all started moving again along with the other refugees.

We were afraid to take the main road any further, so we turned onto a small gravel road that wound into the jungle. We were still focused on getting to Kismayo, which bordered Kenya in southern Somalia. Even though the weather was hot, I felt cold from fear, hunger, thirst, exhaustion, and the knowledge that I was alone now, without any family to protect me. Now that a little time had passed, I was angry that my mother had left without me. I would have left Mogadishu long ago if my mother hadn't refused to go. She'd taken advantage of me so that I'd stay with her, and then she'd abandoned me at the first opportunity.

These thoughts made me feel colder still, even though I was sweating profusely. My long, curly hair irritated me because it hung loose over my shoulders as I ran and frequently got caught in tree branches on the sides of the road, which forced me to stop and untangle myself. "Wait, wait!" I cried out several times. I was afraid the men would leave me because I was slowing them down or because my high summer sandals made too much noise as they slapped against the ground.

Kamaal's sisters were having worse problems than I was. Their clothing and hair were also getting tangled in the jungle trees, but they moved much more slowly than I did, and they paused often and complained about everything—the heat, the jungle, their sore feet, the lack of food and water. I could tell that the girls weren't used to much exercise and the exertion of so much walking and running was taking a toll on them. I quickly grew tired of their childish complaining and resistance, but Kamaal and Josef were patient with them and tried to keep them moving.

Finally, near midnight, after several hours of walking through the trees and hiding in them, we arrived at the beach. I threw off my sandals and ran on my bare feet in the cool sand.

Kamaal and Josef's sisters sat under a tree to cool off. They were breathing as heavily as dogs. Eventually, the girls decided that Kamaal and Josef should go ahead without them. They wanted to stay under the tree and later they would return to Mogadishu. I wasn't sure how the girls thought they could make it back to Mogadishu on their own, but I didn't say anything.

Kamaal and Josef tried to persuade their sisters. "Come now, come now," Kamaal said, crouching down beside them under the tree. "Look at that girl there," and he pointed to me. "If she can go on you can too, come now."

The two girls glanced over at me and then back at their brothers. "No, you two go," one of the sisters said. "We can't. Save yourselves. You're men. It's dangerous to be a man during wartime."

The girls started to cry, which caused Kamaal and Josef to start crying as well. The boys wanted to honor their mother's request and look after their sisters, but it was becoming clear that was impossible. "If you stay with them, you die too," one of the men in our group muttered to Kamaal and Josef. "Come with us now."

Kamaal and Josef looked worried and despondent, but they eventually agreed. "See you in Kismayo," Josef said.

"We'll come back for you," Kamaal promised. "We'll find you, wherever you are."

The girls nodded and wept some more. I turned away for a moment, unable to watch them say goodbye to each other. The war was tearing everyone's family apart. I hadn't even gotten a chance to say goodbye to my brothers and Diina.

Eventually, we moved on and left the girls under the tree on the beach. Kamaal and Josef sniffed and wiped at their eyes but were otherwise quiet. I sensed they knew they would never see their sisters again. They were staying behind in an area heavily populated by the Hawiye clan.

Now I was the only girl left in a group of six men. Since all the men knew my family to some degree, I was comfortable with them even if I didn't fully trust them to stick with me. Four of the men were young, including Kamaal and Josef, but two of the men were about 30-

40 years old, had fought for Siyaad Barre's government, and had guns hidden under their clothes. They'd been in uniform while they were fighting the Hawiye and Ishaaq clans, but when they realized they'd lost the battle, they had taken off their uniforms and were now wearing ridiculous outfits. An overweight man whose name I didn't know was wearing women's clothing—a dress and a couple of shirts. A man by the name of Moses had an orange woman's scarf tied around his waist and was wearing a white T-shirt and a pair of woman's sandals. The younger men were also dressed strangely. Both Josef and Kamaal had left the university in haste and were still wearing pajamas. Another young man, Kamaal and Josef's cousin, had a sheet wrapped around his body, and the final one wore a garbage collector's uniform. As for myself, I wore a pair of green leggings and an untucked skirt. We were all trying to disguise that we belonged to Siyaad Barre's clan.

When we reached at a high sand dune, I glanced back over my shoulder at Mogadishu and saw a huge red fire burning, a sharp contrast to the night sky and the black sea. The flames were engulfing the entire city. I shuddered at the thought of someone still trapped down there while the city burned.

Our goal was to reach a road where we could catch a lift to Kismayo. We had been walking for so many hours that we could hardly walk anymore because our feet were so sore. But there was nothing else to do but keep moving. None of us had drunk any water all day. Also, though we were alone and there were no people in sight, we were still afraid that someone was coming after us. We all knew people from the Hawiye clan lived all around Mogadishu. Long before the war had broken out at the capital, they'd moved with their families out into the bush and to villages where they lived in small military camps while they plotted the coup against Siyaad Baare. Now we were in the bush, in Hawiye territory. If we heard voices or the approach of footsteps, we would hide under a tree or behind some bushes and speak only in very low voices. The stress of our situation was catching up to me. I was worried that we were lost and there was no one to turn to for help.

We walked for another four hours in the dry countryside. I noticed that Josef walked crookedly, and one leg was shorter than the other, which always threatened to make him lose his balance. Finally, exhausted, we stopped to camp under a bunch of trees that stood in the middle of a line of bushes. I sat down beside Kamaal because I trusted him more than anyone else in the group. "Please don't leave me while I sleep," I whispered to him.

He looked at me with surprise. "I can still run and walk," I continued. "If we get caught, I'll deny I've ever seen you or Josef before."

I wanted Kamaal to see me as a strong member of the group and not as a burden. "I won't leave you," Kamaal said calmly. "I promised your mother to help you."

Eventually, we all lay down and tried to rest, but I couldn't sleep. The ground was hard and rocky, and my throat was starting to burn from the lack of water. Also, despite Kamaal's reassuring words, I was still afraid the men might abandon me while I slept. Since I was the only woman, they might see me as someone who would slow them up. I was afraid to close my eyes and mostly stayed awake the entire night, keeping an eye out on the men. If any of them stirred or stood up to go to the bathroom, I was suspicious and thought they were planning to leave.

When the sun began to rise, we stood up and quietly continued through the bush like weary soldiers. Soon we reached cultivated fields with sugar cane, corn, and watermelon. Unfortunately, the crops weren't ripe yet and didn't offer us any food. Despite our night of sleep, the fat man wearing the woman's dress was still very tired. Finally, he lay down under an acacia tree with his rifle by his side.

"Go on without me," he said in a defeated voice. "I can't go any farther."

He was saying the exact same thing as Kamaal and Josef's sisters had said. Again, people in our group tried to talk the man into continuing with us. "Come on," Kamaal said. "You can handle going the rest of the way. We can take more small breaks if you want."

But the man was determined. His feet ached and were soaked, and he couldn't walk. He sounded defeated and ready to accept his fate. Eventually, we had to leave him behind. Like Kamaal and Josef's sisters, he wasn't physically fit enough for a long journey, and in the end, we all wanted to survive. We couldn't continue forward with someone who couldn't walk. Later, I heard this man had been killed by the Hawiye clan.

Now our group was down to me and five guys. We continued moving and tried to ignore our exhaustion. It was nine o'clock and the sun was rising higher. Already it was very hot even though it was still midmorning. I stared at the stark trees we passed, their dry arms sticking up into the sky.

The path we were on became wider, and suddenly we heard voices coming from a field. We came across a man standing in the middle of the sandy road. We greeted him politely, but he looked back at us with suspicion. It turned out that he knew Moses. They were not friends but had worked together many years ago.

"Where are you going?" the man asked, looking contemptuously at the orange woman's scarf Moses had tied around his waist.

We looked at each other in silence, unsure how much we could tell this man. "We're going to visit some family in Afgooye," Kamaal said. That was a lie but a necessary one. If we told this man we were headed for Kismayo, he could guess we were trying to flee into Kenya and figure out we were from the Darod clan. "There's a lot of trouble back in Mogadishu," Kamaal added.

The man nodded. I couldn't tell if he believed us or not. "It's a long way to Afgooye," he said. "It's dangerous for you to walk through the fields like this. There could be people from the Hawiye clan around." He paused and then added, "Follow me. You can get something to drink at my camp."

We were hesitant to return to the man's camp because we knew he was probably from the Hawiye clan and was lying to us in the same way we were lying to him. But we didn't have any choice. If we tried to run away from him, it would prove we were afraid and signal that we were from the Darod clan. As we followed the man to his camp, Kamaal whispered to us that we could never admit that we were from the Darod clan. We should say we were from different clans so that if one of us was recognized and killed, the rest of us still would have a chance to survive. We all agreed.

When the armed guards at the entrance to the camp saw us, they approached us angrily. "Where are you going? they demanded.

We all froze. The man who had invited us said, "I know him" and pointed at Moses. "I want to give them something to drink. They've been walking a long time."

The guards squinted at us and then looked at Moses. "He has to hand over his gun first," one of the guards said.

After Moses surrendered his gun, we were allowed to enter the camp. We passed many dilapidated tents with women and children sitting outside. They stared as us as if we were from another world. Finally, we stopped at a large acacia tree. A big group of men, both young and old, were standing and sitting under the tree. They looked at me and then gave me permission to join their women, who were sitting under a nearby tree and making food. They had large knives and razor blades in their hands as they cut up meat.

"No, I'll stay here," I said timidly. I was too afraid to separate from the group I'd come with.

The men under the tree laughed at me. "Your choice," they said in a superior tone.

I sat down next to Kamaal and Josef. I decided to stay close to my group until I found my own family. "No, she must come over to us!" the women cried. "We will take care of her."

Still, I shook my head. The knives and the razors made me nervous. I was a little afraid they'd cut me with the blades. I glanced over at Kamaal and Josef, but their heads were bowed passively. None of the men in my group were making eye contact with anyone. I did the same thing.

We were served rice, boiled meat, and tea with camel milk. Moses and the young man wearing the sheet ate their food, but Kamaal and Josef sat quietly and didn't eat, and I was too scared to eat. We were worried that we were in danger and the man had brought us back to his camp to kill us. We knew Moses, and that was proof enough that we belonged to their enemies. I hid behind Kamaal and kept thinking: *Now they will shoot us right here while we eat.*

Among the men was the leader of one of Somalia's regions. He was only about forty years old but looked much older. He was small and thin with no teeth. When he talked, he stammered, which made it hard to understand him. He squinted often and his eyes didn't focus in the same direction. He said he knew the Darod clan inside and out, that he hated Siyaad Barre and his regime and felt that everyone from the Darod clan deserved to be shot. He stood up and looked at all of us with fierce eyes. "Which clan do you come from?" he asked us.

I was terrified by the question but knew enough not to answer him directly. Instead, we mentioned we came from several different clans, but none of us mentioned Barre's clan. It was humiliating and degrading to be treated as subhuman because of your clan, but we all knew that if we wanted to survive, we had to deny who we really were.

"You look like someone who comes from Siyaad Barre's clan," he said, pointing to me.

A young man stood up, took out his rifle, and with an evil grin placed the barrel of the gun against my neck. "I want to shoot you first," he said. "You are a woman. It would be a shame if you have to watch all your friends die."

I closed my eyes and waited for him to pull the trigger. He pushed the barrel of the rifle, hard, against my neck for a long time as he talked to the others about how to shoot us. Kamaal, Josef, and the other men in my group remained silent and continued to stare down at the ground. The man with the rifle was trying to provoke our group by singling me out and threatening me so the men would react. But Kamaal and the others were determined not to challenge them and start a fight. We'd all be dead for sure if that happened.

I grew dizzy and light-headed from the force of the gun against my neck. Finally, one of the men from the Hawiye tribe said, "Stop now. Step away from the girl."

The young man leered at me once more. "I would like to keep you for myself," he said, pulled the rifle away and lowered it back to his side.

I fainted. I'm not sure how long I blacked out. When I came to, my body was numb and I couldn't feel anything, but I could hear the men talking. I was in a strange state, still not sure if I was dead or alive. An older man came over to me, said hello, and seemed about to ask me, in my disoriented state, what clan I was from. Kamaal nudged me and I came fully awake and was conscious again.

Even though I no longer had a gun pointed at my neck, I still felt powerless. Everyone in my group continued to deny coming from the Darod clan, which was the only thing they were interested in knowing. I was also nervous that the young man with the gun would decide to keep me, and I wouldn't be allowed to leave with Kamaal and Josef and the rest. And how could anyone stop the young man from keeping me if he decided he wanted to?

Late in the afternoon, several men in the camp said we could all leave except for Moses. They insisted that Moses had to stay behind with them because of his past work with Barre. A camp guide and Moses's former work companion followed us away from the camp. Moses was only allowed to follow us for part of the way before he was forced to turn back. I was scared for Moses, who was forty and had three children and a wife waiting for him somewhere. When we were walking out of the camp and before Moses had to return to the Hawiye camp, he said to me, low so no one else could hear: "Maybe you will survive because you are a girl. Maybe I will not survive. Tell my wife I was arrested by the Hawiye clan. I think your mother knows my wife."

We said goodbye to Moses, who was left with tears in his eyes and a blank expression on his face. To this day, I don't know what happened to him. I don't know if his wife was ever told that he'd been arrested by the Hawiye clan. I never found out her name and could never deliver Moses's message to her.

The guide escorted us further away from the camp. We were told that we must not speak while walking through the countryside, as many people lived in the bush and wandered the fields, and we could easily be killed. When we reached the road, the guide told us we would have to continue the rest of the way on our own. We thanked him for the food and his help.

However, we did not think that we had completely gotten away from the Hawiye. We still thought there was a chance more Hawiye would come after us. And that is what happened. After the guide left us, we walked on our own for a while before we ran across four young men from the Hawiye clan. There were several Hawiye camps all over the area, so the young men could have come from a different camp nearby, or maybe they were from the camp we'd just left. The young men were all armed and looked at us in a scornful, threatening way. "There's no way out for you," one of the young men said. "You'll have to go back to Mogadishu."

He told me to cross to the other side of the road. "The rest of you stay here," he said.

By now my whole body was probably shaking, but I only remember the trembling of my head and hands. I was sure we were all going to die, and I couldn't bear the thought of watching Kamaal and Josef and the others get shot in front of me. "If you're going to kill us, then I want to be first," I said hoarsely.

The young men stared at me. "We won't shoot you," one of them said. "We'll keep you as a slave."

"A slave?" This was a word we didn't normally use in Somalia. "What do you mean?"

"You will get plenty of work," he said with a twisted smile. "You will cook for us, wash our clothes, and have sex with us whenever we want. If you refuse, we will kill you."

"Sex?" I was taken aback. "Aren't you Muslims?"

"Darod women do not deserve respect," he said, and the young man and his friends laughed.

I felt horrified and defeated. I would rather die than get passed around the Hawiye tribe as a sex slave. "You can shoot me first," I repeated.

Two older men came down the road from the direction we'd just come. These were men I recognized who had been eating with us under the large acacia tree in the camp. They came over to us and angrily asked the young men, "What are you doing? Don't shoot anyone."

At first, the young men were defiant. "They're ours!" one of the young men said, pointing to me and the others in my group.

"No," one of the old men said and began to scold the younger men. They argued back and forth, the old men saying, "Away with you! Go away with you! You must not do anything stupid."

Reluctantly, the young men whispered between themselves, then lowered their weapons and walked off. As it turned out, they were from the camp we had just left. One of the old men told us that the young men were waiting to ambush us once the guide had left us.

To make sure that we were safe, the older men followed us down the road for a while so that the young men could not turn back and harass us again. Everyone in my group cried, shaken by the violent behavior and how close we'd come to getting killed. Eventually, the old men turned around to head back to their camp. We thanked them for their help and for saving our lives. When evening arrived, we finally reached the main road leading to Kismayo.

There weren't any cars on the road, and we were completely exhausted, so we sat down on the side of the road, hoping someone would drive by. After fifteen minutes, an old decrepit pickup with four people in the front seat pulled to a stop. The driver rolled down his window. Immediately, we saw that several of the men held rifles, AK-47s, and looked ready to use them if we made any threatening moves. "Have you heard that the government of Siyaad Barre has resigned?" the driver asked.

We answered yes, and I immediately said we were heading to Afgooye to visit friends and family. We couldn't admit we were trying to get to Kismayo for fear we'd get shot. "We'll bring you to Afgooye," the driver said, "but you should also come with us to Mogadishu. We're celebrating our new freedom."

Return to Mogadishu after we'd walked all this way to escape from it? But we couldn't say no because they had so many guns and looked like they were high on khat. We also could tell, by their dialect and their dress, not to mention their desire to "celebrate their new freedom," that the men in the truck were from the Hawiye clan, driving up and down that road to Kismayo in search of anyone from the Darod clan. Reluctantly, we hopped up onto the bed of the truck.

After an hour we arrived on the outskirts of Afgooye, located over eighteen miles south of Mogadishu. The men stopped the pickup and told us they needed to buy coke and cigarettes to go with the khat.

"I have an aunt who lives here," I said. "I want to visit her and present my husband to her."

I grabbed hold of Kamaal's hand so the men in the pickup would understand that he was my husband. Kamaal accepted the lie and didn't say a word. He knew this was a survival strategy. I couldn't save them all, but I thought I had to try and save one or two. There was no question in my mind that I would choose to save Kamaal over anyone else. I'd developed a stronger relationship with him during the short amount of time we'd been together, and he was the one in the group who was most attentive to my needs. Kamaal told the other men in the group to slow down if they were walking too fast for me to keep up, and it was Kamaal who suggested occasional breaks so that I'd have a chance to rest and regain my strength. He was the one who gave me food and kept me up to date on what was going on. Sometimes he sang to us and told a lot of stories to keep us upbeat and help us from getting discouraged. He made it clear through his actions that he didn't intend to leave me behind. Sometimes we laughed together, sometimes we cried, and we dreamed together about surviving the war and having the opportunity to start a new life.

The men in the pickup gave me permission to go with Kamaal to meet my aunt. Emboldened, I lied again and said that I had borrowed some money from one of the other men and that I would pay him back if he joined us now. I pointed to Josef because he was Kamaal's brother, and I wanted to help him survive too, if possible. I didn't have a strong relationship with Josef, but I knew he was weak and fragile and his chances of surviving on his own, apart from Kamaal, were slim. Besides, if I left Kamaal's brother behind, would Kamaal decide to leave me?

The driver looked doubtfully at me. "Okay," he said. "But the other two stay here with us."

Kamaal and Josef's cousin and the young man wearing the trash collector's uniform looked over at us with fear and regret, but they also understood we had to get away if we could. Kamaal, Josef, and I walked across the road and hid ourselves behind some grass and an old palm tree. From there, we watched the pickup. Kamaal's cousin and the other young man were sitting on the roof of the truck, and we hoped they'd manage to escape from the men in the pickup so that we could all escape together.

There was a river that ran from Afgooye to Kismayo. "Maybe we should hide in the water," I told Kamaal.

Kamaal shook his head. "We can't," he said. "There are hippos and crocodiles and snakes in that water. Forget it."

"What about if we just walk along the river?" I asked. "The river leads to Kismayo."

But Kamaal said this was also not a good idea. "There are dangerous animals near the river too," he said, still staring across the road at the pickup. "It's not safe near the river."

"Okay," I said and dropped the idea.

The streets were chaotic, filled with donkeys, cars, and people on foot passing over the bridge. People from the Darod clan were heading south towards Kismayo, and the other clans were heading towards Mogadishu. Some were carrying their possessions in their hands or strapped to their backs. Others hurried along with nothing. Kamaal, Josef, and I remained hidden, still hoping that our friends would break away from the men in the pickup.

Then shooting started nearby. Suddenly, the pickup exploded into flames. The air grew black with smoke. People started yelling and screaming. We stood shocked for a moment, then Kamaal ran across the road while Josef and I followed. Kamaal stood next to the burning vehicle and shouted his cousin's name.

"Kamaal, stop!" Josef yelled and held Kamaal back. "You'll get yourself killed too."

"What the hell is happening?" Kamaal said, in tears. "What's happening in this country?"

I comforted Kamaal as best as I could. "We have to go now," I said, "or we'll all be dead too."

Kamaal pulled himself together, and the three of us started running away. We had no idea where we were going. We were moving on animal instinct, trying to survive.

We ran along with a bunch of others down the road that led into Afgooye. Once we were inside the city, we tried to hide in abandoned houses and shacks so we wouldn't be recognized as members of the Darod clan.

Finally, we saw an old, red truck filled with people as it drove slowly through the city. We ran up to the truck. "Where are you going?" Kamaal asked.

"Kismayo," the driver said.

"Can we get a ride?" I asked, excited. "We can pay you when we reach Kismayo."

The driver's face hardened. "If you do not pay now, it will not be possible to go with us," he said.

The strain was too much, and I broke into tears. I asked several times for the driver to let us ride with the rest of the truckload of people to Kismayo. "This is our only chance to survive," I told him. "Our family is waiting for us in Kismayo."

Eventually, the driver yielded and said I could ride with the others. "But what about them?" I asked and pointed at Kamaal and Josef.

Kamaal and Josef looked down and said nothing. They knew that if they said anything, the driver would refuse them, but it was harder for the driver to refuse me, a woman. They didn't want to interfere with my chance at safety. And yet I felt I couldn't leave them behind. "These are my brothers!" I cried out. They'd come to feel like brothers to me through this ordeal we were going through. "I cannot leave them."

The driver scowled at me. "That's your problem," he said.

I ran around the truck begging, crying, and praying to the others on the truck to help us and give us some money if they could. The passengers looked sad and helpless, and many of them looked down to avoid making eye contact with me. A few women cried because they couldn't help me. Most of the passengers were afraid to say anything to the driver because he could throw them off the truck for the slightest provocation. An old lady said to the driver, "Can't we take the kids with us? They can pay you in Kismayo." But the driver said no to her as well, and the old woman didn't dare to press him any further.

I hurried back to the driver. "Do you know Mohammed Hirsi?" I asked. "He lives in Kismayo. He's the director of an oil and gas company. He's my mother's cousin. We will be living with him, and you can get your money from him."

The driver laughed bitterly. "We've heard that story before," he said.

I didn't know what else to say to him. I gave up, and Kamaal, Josef, and I sat down on the roadside and watched the last of the people climb onto the truck before it drove off and disappeared. We were exhausted and too shaken by the chaos and the death of Kamaal and Josef's cousin and the other young man to talk to each other and try to lift each other's spirits. Everything was happening so fast and there was no time to focus on anything other than survival. I felt fragile and orphaned. I realized that Somalia no longer operated under any sort of laws and norms. People ran wild and did what they wanted to: killing, burning houses, seeking revenge on real and imagined enemies. We were an outlaw country now and trying to escape it felt impossible.

The day was getting late, and we had not eaten since the day before. My stomach was empty, and I occasionally felt faint and light-headed from the hunger. I was worried also about where we would sleep that night. Suddenly, another old truck pulled up to the side of the road, also jammed with people trying to escape. We ran over to the truck and asked if we could go with them.

Two men who worked for the driver and helped people get on and off the truck looked at us harshly. "Why don't you want to go to Mogadishu?" one of them asked.

The mention of Mogadishu made me fear they were from the Hawiye clan. They were teasing and laughing at me because they could see how desperate we all were. I was humiliated every time one of the men laughed or sneered at me. Was there no end to this madness? Kamaal and Josef were again quiet. Since I was a woman, they knew I had a better chance of convincing the men to let us come along than they had.

"We have friends who are getting married tomorrow in Kismayo," I told them. The lie came easily off my tongue. Lying was the only way to survive in this mad world. "After the wedding, we will return to Mogadishu."

I wasn't sure if the men believed me, but the fact I spoke with a Mogadishu dialect helped make my lie seem plausible. "The cost is $300 for all three of you," the driver said.

We went through the same process we had with the previous driver. We told him we had no money with us but would pay him when we arrived in Kismayo.

The driver shook his head vigorously. "No, that won't work. You must pay now."

I knew that if I left Kamaal and Josef, they would have a difficult time surviving. They were decent and intellectual students who were out of their element in a civil war where people shot each other so easily. Because they were young men, the risk of someone killing them was greater than it was for me. And I was better at begging and trying to negotiate with men than either Kamaal and Josef were. We had to find some way to pay for a ride to Kismayo. I was wearing Diina's small gold chain that I removed from my neck. Briefly, I wondered how I would explain to her, if I ever saw her again, that I'd given her gold necklace away, but the situation now was too extreme to worry about such small things. Kamaal and Josef had a watch that they offered to the driver, but they didn't know how much it was worth.

"This is all we have," I told the driver, handing him the watch and the gold chain. "We will pay the rest when we come to Kismayo."

The driver looked at our stuff and laughed. "This is not enough," he sneered. "You can't buy a ride with this cheap junk."

Once again, I threw out my arms, begging, praying, and crying. Again, I told the story of my mother's cousin in Kismayo and asked if the driver knew him.

The driver's eyes lit up slightly. "I have heard of Mohammed Hirsi," he said. "He is a rich man."

"Yes," I said, relieved, seizing on a sliver of hope. "We'll be staying with him, all three of us. You will get your money once we arrive."

The driver paused a moment and considered. He turned and whispered to a man sitting beside him in the truck. "If you leave the truck without paying, we will kill you," he said.

Then he motioned for us to hop up onto the roof of his truck. Kamaal and Josef went up first and then helped pull me up. I felt alive again, my blood surging with promise.

We drove from Afgooye toward Kismayo. After four hours, the driver said he and his associates were going to sleep in the next town, called Jamaame, because they were tired. We asked to stay in the truck because we were afraid they would drive off and leave us if we weren't right there when they decided to leave in the morning.

When we were driving outside the city boundary of Jamaame, we were shot at directly. Bullets zinged past us. Kamaal, Josef, and I threw ourselves flat on the cab roof. The bullets cracked into the old truck's metal sides. Because it was a dark and desolate area, we couldn't see who was shooting at us.

"We are civilians!" we shouted. "We have no firearms!"

A man sitting on the edge of the truck was shot. His body dropped back down on people who were sitting on the truck's bed. People yelled and screamed. A woman cried out, "Help him! Help him!"

Eventually, a man jumped off the truck and began to run haphazardly toward the spot where the shots were coming from. "We're ordinary passengers going to Kismayo!" he shouted with his hands raised in the air to show he wasn't armed.

The shooting stopped then. The people shooting were from the Darod clan and had thought we were their enemies. The truck drove on. My body was shaking as I checked my arms, legs, chest, to make sure I hadn't been hit. Nausea overwhelmed me, and I had to duck my head over the side of the cab so I could throw up. The bitter taste of vomit burned in my mouth and throat. The man who'd been shot was bleeding profusely, but we didn't have anything in the truck to help stop the bleeding. We stopped in a small town, and someone climbed off the truck with the man to take him to the doctor. The rest of us stayed on the truck.

Soon we reached Jamaame. When the truck stopped, I was finally able to sleep, although sleeping on the roof of a truck was not comfortable, especially with so many other people around. I had nightmares and my brain was constantly racing. Sometimes I had flashbacks that I couldn't tell apart from a nightmare. I was exhausted but could only sleep for small periods of time before my body jolted away again.

Early the next morning, I woke up, disoriented. It was time to drive on. Kamaal, Josef, and I sat up, still tired, our clothes dusty and sweaty. The road was guarded by members of Siyaad Barre's military regime and his supporters from the Darod clan, and the truck was stopped several times while we were interrogated. Had we run into any of their enemies from the Ishaaq or Hawiye clan while we were driving? What clan were we from? Could we prove it? Each time we were asked these questions, it was hard to convince the soldiers that we came from the Darod clan and were not their enemies.

I didn't mind telling these soldiers I was from the Darod clan, but mostly I kept my clan affiliation to myself. I lived in dread that I would run into someone who would betray me and identify me as someone from the Darod clan. In Somalia, ordinary citizens who were politically aware was commonplace. Many took an active part in the civil war. You could no longer trust anyone. I remember that some of our neighbors, for example, who were sweet and helpful for years before the civil war, turned on us once the war broke out. The change was sudden and extreme: people killed their neighbors and betrayed their friends if they came from the Darod clan. Being a member of the Darod clan had become a death sentence.

Eventually, the truck reached a small, dusty town so people could climb out for some water and to go to the bathroom. But the village was so tiny there were no more than ten houses. I needed to find a toilet, so I walked down the road a bit until I ran across a small shop where they sold food and cigarettes. When I reached the door, I saw that the clerk was a girl from the Hawiye clan who had been in my high school class. Quickly, I turned away and ran back to the truck. I was carrying a shawl along with me to cover my head if it got too hot, and now I tossed the shawl over me so that only my eyes were visible.

"Did you find a toilet?" Kamaal asked when I returned.

I explained what had happened. "But she doesn't know you," I said. "You can use the bathroom if you want to."

Instead, they walked to the other side of the road and urinated in the grass. I was envious of their freedom. It was harder for women to find a way to pee. I had to sneak off behind a tree or some grass. I was afraid of reptiles and always made to make sure I didn't pee on a snake. At night, I could just pee in the middle of a road since there were no people around and never much traffic. Not only was it simpler for men to go to the bathroom, but, unlike women, men didn't have to fear getting raped or abused as a sex slave. I had nightmares about getting raped by one or more men. Maybe they would cut me up first because I was circumcised; I had heard this was a common practice of rapists. Because I was young and unmarried, I was attractive prey. I learned later that one of my cousins was one of many girls who was raped during the civil war. She and I had gone to school together, but after her rape she no longer recognized me or anyone. Her rape had been particularly brutal. She had been raped and abused by many different men for an entire month. The weeks of torture had driven her insane, destroying her both physically and mentally. Her family had to look after her as if she were a child.

Because of the many military checkpoints along the way, it took us a whole day to travel from Jamaame to Kismayo. Usually, that trip only took a few hours. The closer we got to Kismayo, the more uneasy I grew about paying for the trip. The truck driver had ordered us to remain seated on the roof of the cab until the other passengers had gotten off. Also, I couldn't remember where my mother's cousin lived. I had only visited him at his place once, so I was trying very hard to remember how to get to his place.

Eventually, we entered the city. Once, Kismayo had been a big, beautiful place with many traders, orchards, and cosmopolitan attractions. Now the city was filled with refugees from Mogadishu. People who had previously lived in large houses and driven around in luxurious cars were now living in the streets. It was just another grim change the war had brought about.

Since I wasn't sure how to direct the driver, I asked him if he knew where Mohammed Hirsi lived, and fortunately he said yes. I was briefly relieved.

But when we got to Mohammed's house, no one was home. An elderly woman who was keeping an eye on the neighborhood told us the Hirsi family had fled the previous week to Afmadow, a town on the Somalia-Kenya border.

I didn't know what to say to the driver. I could see he was getting angry. "What now?" he asked me in a terse voice. "How are you going to pay for your ride?"

I just looked down at the ground, speechless. "Maybe we can drive into town," Josef suggested. "We can look for our family and friends."

But neither the driver nor his associates were enthusiastic about that proposal. "I don't feel like driving all over the city looking for your relatives," the driver complained. "It's not my responsibility, and it would cost a lot of money for the gasoline." He thought for a moment, then told us he'd drive us to the city center and then we must find someone who could pay what we owed him.

We were exhausted by the lack of food and sleep but felt we had no choice and had to agree. When we reached the city center, the driver ordered two of us to stay behind next to the truck while the other one went out to find some money. After a brief discussion, we agreed that Kamaal should go.

While Kamaal was away, Josef and I stayed in the truck. After two hours, I started to worry that Kamaal might not come back at all. The driver was growing impatient. He decided to go into a restaurant and eat with one of his helpers while the other helper stayed out with us and guarded the truck with a gun so that we wouldn't run away.

Josef and I were tense and restless while alone inside the truck. "What should we do if Kamaal doesn't come back or can't get the money?" I whispered to Josef.

He told me to sit somewhere in the truck where it would be easy to jump down and run away. "If anyone runs after you, scream loudly like you're crazy and people should hear you," Josef said. "Say the man is trying to rape you. Or say he's from the Hawiye clan and caught you on the street while you were trying to visit your uncle. Everyone here knows your uncle. And there are a lot of people from the Darod clan here with guns, waiting to defend people from the Hawiye."

Josef's plan made sense to me. Maybe I'd underestimated him, I thought. Maybe he was a lot smarter than I'd been giving him credit for. I smiled at him, but then saw the man outside the truck with his gun, looking in at us. I stopped smiling and did my best to look docile.

When another hour had passed, the driver and his cohort returned, well-fed and happy. The driver smoked a cigarette, smiled a little, and asked his helper, "Didn't that boy come back yet?"

The man shook his head. "No," one of them said. "We don't think he is going to come back, either."

The driver's happiness soon disappeared. He opened the truck door so he could speak to us directly. "You are both so stupid!" he shouted at us. "Did you really think your friend would come back with money to help you when he can just run off on his own."

"He'll come back," Josef insisted.

"Stupid young kids! You don't know anything about what's going on. You are street kids who steal and lie a lot." He turned toward me. "You don't have any family and no money either," he said, his voice rising even louder. "It was all a lie."

"He will come back," Josef said again. "We are sure of it. He would never leave us behind."

"Yes, he won't leave us behind." Now more than ever, I needed to maintain my faith in Kamaal.

The driver said he was tired of waiting. "We have to take on some new passengers now," he said. "You two will drive back to Afgooye with us since you have not paid for this trip."

Return to Afgooye without Kamaal? We had just come from Afgooye two days ago! I was frightened and frustrated and started crying again. How could people be so cruel when it was a matter of life or death? I prayed to Allah for help, although I wasn't sure by then why I kept praying. Allah had forgotten and abandoned me.

"Please," I said to the driver. "Just twenty more minutes."

Stubbornly, the driver shook his head. "No more waiting," he said. "I make money by driving people. The more waiting, the less I make."

"Isn't driving around in a civil war dangerous?" I was desperate and trying to stall for time.

He smiled at me, but it was a resigned smile. "If I die, I die," he said. "I will have to die at some point anyway. But if I am going to live for a long time, I do not want to live in poverty and fear."

I explained our situation to him, hoping for some mercy. We did not want to return to Afgooye for any reason. "If we ride with you, we could be shot," I said.

"It's better to die than to live in hiding." He sounded both fearless and despairing.

I wondered then if it would be so bad to die. Maybe it was preferable to having to suffer endlessly like this?

At that moment, Kamaal rounded a corner with two men and approached the truck. He had not seen anyone from their family or mine, but he had borrowed money from some acquaintances. Josef and I cheered and grabbed hold of each other's hands in relief. It felt like we had been in jail, awaiting execution. Now we were free!

The Cafe Owner

After the hell we went through to get to Kismayo, Kamaal, Josef and I recommitted to sticking together until we found our families. First, we had to find a place where we could spend the night. Although Kamaal had also borrowed money to buy us supper from the same people who had given him money to pay the truck driver, we did not know where to spend the night or how we would be able to get food the next day. We walked through town to find the cheapest place to eat. We had a total of 200 Somalian shillings. We wanted to spend 100 shillings for dinner and save the other 100 shillings for the next day.

We ran across a cosy café near the beach that was run by a young man named Bashi. He was an attractive man with light black skin and very gravelly hair. He didn't belong to any clan, which made us like and trust him more than we did most strangers. Although Bashi's dialect was difficult for us to understand, we chatted with him and learned he'd been born and raised in Kismayo. His family owned the entire house and lived on the top floor above the café. Everyone except Bashi and his mother had moved out to a nearby island because of the war. His father had died a year earlier and Bashi had inherited his father's small fishing boat. Bashi's two sisters were married, and his wife was pregnant and currently living with her family to give birth. Her family lived in a small fishing village on the Kenyan border, so Bashi could also speak Swahili. His grandparents made a living by sailing back and forth, doing business with traders in Kenya.

"Where do you live?" he asked, since he could tell we were not from Kismayo.

We told him we lived in Mogadishu. "There are many refugees in the city from Mogadishu," Bashi said. "It is a very difficult situation for you to be in." He paused and then asked, "What would you like to eat?"

We stared silently out the window into the busy street. None of us wanted to say we only had 100 shillings we could offer for food. He looked at us with compassion. "Don't you have any money?" he asked.

Tears welled in my eyes, but I was too tired to break down and cry. "We only have 200 shillings to last us until we find our family," I told him.

"Give me 100 shillings and I'll get you some food," he said.

Bashi made us a meal of fish, liver, and potatoes. We were so hungry that we could hardly eat anything. We sat at a table inside the café. A couple of tribal customers were sitting at other tables, and they glanced over at us curiously. I heard one of the customers asking Bashi who we were and where we came from. "They're my friends from Mogadishu," Bashi replied.

When we were finished with our meal, Bashi offered us each a cup of tea. It was the nicest cup of tea I'd ever had. Finally, we stood up from the table and said goodbye to the sweet young man. "Where are you going to spend the night?" he asked.

When we admitted we didn't know, he said, "You can sleep here tonight if you would like."

His offer was tempting, but we wanted to go out exploring in Kismayo and search for our family and acquaintances first. We told Bashi that if we didn't find anyone, we would return to his café.

Kamaal, Josef, and I walked toward the city center and felt very unsafe. You could never tell if a bomb would suddenly explode or if someone would run up and take you prisoner. We did not see many people we knew, and those we did recognize and talked to said they had not seen our families. Eventually, we returned to Bashi's café, and he seemed pleased to see us. He said I should sleep in a small office room that was used as a guest room, and the boys should sleep in the hallway on the carpeted floor. This was the best sleeping arrangement we'd had since we fled Mogadishu.

Bashi did not wake us up the next morning and let us sleep in until 3:00 pm. When we were finally awake, we saw he'd prepared a lot of food for us—camel meat and rice with sauce and chili, all which was traditional Somalian food. While we'd been sleeping, Bashi had gone into town to buy food he thought we would prefer over fish and liver. He insisted that we didn't need to pay him for the food. Kamaal, Josef and I ate as much as we could without becoming sick. After the meal, we washed ourselves in a small shower that Bashi had outside the back of the house and started to feel like human beings again. We offered to help Bashi clean up, but he said we were his guests and should take it easy. Bashi also offered to let us stay with him until we found our families. His kindness and generosity were a godsend after several days of stress from fighting for our lives.

Since we had free time now as well as a place to stay, Kamaal, Josef and I walked down to the white sandy beach and watched the big waves roll in. This, too, felt like a luxury. Eventually, we talked about what we would do if we couldn't find our families. "We should go to Kenya," I told them. "It will be safe there."

But Kamaal and Josef pointed out we didn't have enough money or passports, so we couldn't travel to another country. "It's easier for us to stay here in Kismayo," Kamaal said.

I wasn't sure if I agreed, but I didn't say any more about that. I didn't dare leave the boys and go off on my own. "I will stay with you both until I find my family," I said.

"Of course," Kamaal said.

While I'd chosen to stay with Kamaal and Josef, I also decided I should keep my options open about Kenya. When we returned to Bashi's place, we asked him if anyone was sailing to Kenya, and he gave us a lot of information. He said we had two transportation options. One, we could walk sixty miles to the Kenyan border, which would take us about two days. But this was a very risky and dangerous venture since there were a lot of clans and subclans in that area. Armed groups in small towns and out in the bush could attack us and shoot us for no other reason than we were from the Darod clan. The second option was for us to sail to Kenya. Bashi believed this was a safer option because the war was taking place on land and not at sea.

It was unusual for me to live with strangers and away from my family for so long. Kamaal and Josef were brothers, I thought enviously, and even though they sometimes fought, they had that family connection to rely on, while I was alone. As often as possible, the three of us went into the city center in search of our families, even though the area was always filled with cars, smoke, and noise. There were more and more wounded people crowding the streets. Many of them cried out and begged for someone to help them. A few lay on the sidewalk and it was impossible to tell if they were alive or dead. I averted my eyes whenever we passed a dead body flattened out on the street. Instead, I focused my attention on the faces of people in the crowds, searching for my mother, or Diina, or Rush or Wali. But I never found them, and Kamaal and Josef never found their mother or their sisters.

Kamaal and Josef still carried around a lot of guilt for leaving their sisters behind in the Hawiye area in the dead of night, even when it had been the girls' idea for Kamaal and Josef to go on without them. Now that the boys were relatively safe, they struggled with their consciences that they'd promised their mother they'd look after their sisters and then hadn't done so. And as we continued to search for our families, without success, both Kamaal and Josef grew more resigned and irritable, especially Josef, who did not like our frequent trips into the city. "We should stop looking for our families," he said once. "They might have fled to the north or are out of the country entirely. They might be dead." A couple of times, Josef refused to go into town with Kamaal and I, and he stayed at the café with Bashi.

One afternoon, when all three of us were in town, Kamaal and Josef were especially grim and silent and didn't talk to each other. I knew there was tension between them, which finally reached a boiling point when Kamaal lashed out at Josef. "You should have stayed with the girls!" he said.

Josef was offended. "*I* should have stayed with them and not you?" he shouted. "What? Why couldn't you stay with them?"

They yelled back and forth for a minute, and then they turned silent again.

When it grew late, we returned to Bashi's place. Now he allowed us to help him with the upkeep of the cafe, and in return, he provided us with food and lodging. I helped him mop the floors and wipe the tables and countertops with a wet cloth. I was responsible for making canjeero and Malawah, thick pancakes fried in oil, a traditional Somalian food. When I was living with my family, I hated cooking, but at Bashi's place, I didn't mind it. I wanted to earn my keep, and I needed to pass the time somehow. Sometimes the boys teased me that Bashi was in love with me, and that was why he was helping us. "That is not true," I said, blushing, whenever the boys brought it up. "You talk to him more than I do."

I could feel that my life was changing and wondered if I would ever get my old, more comfortable life back. Despite the constant tension and oppressiveness of living with my mother, at least I'd had some stability in my life—regular meals and a place to sleep every night. Now everyone in Somalia was insecure and afraid. We didn't know what would happen the next day, next month, next year. Finding food to eat and a place to stay overnight became the primary concerns. In my mind, the same questions came up again and again: *How can I survive? How can I find my family? What future will Somalia have? What will my future be? What should I do tomorrow?*

When three days had passed, the war was only eighteen miles from Kismayo. Despite the war advancing closer, Bashi and the boys were getting along very well and enjoying each other's company. They were all young men and so had a lot in common. I, on the other hand, was lonely a lot of the time. Still, I fell in love with Kismayo when Bashi drove us around town in his small, old Fiat. The city was not as loud, dirty, and filled with people as Mogadishu. Parts of Kismayo had rivers, harbors, and white sandy beaches, and was located close to the Kenyan border. I thought if I survived this civil war, I wouldn't mind living in Kismayo.

As the days passed, I continued to mention to Kamaal and Josef the possibility of leaving town. They continued to resist, although Kamaal showed signs of reconsidering when I talked to him alone while we walked on the beach in search of some nice rocks. At one point, Kamaal suggested that we stay one more week in the city and continue to search for people we knew, and then we could leave. But when Kamaal mentioned this to Josef, Josef said he wanted to stay behind with Bashi and then catch up with us later. We discussed the pros and cons of this for three days. Meanwhile, the war was advancing closer to Kismayo. Kamaal noticed this and confronted Josef about his unwillingness to leave town. "You have to forget about staying here with Bashi," Kamaal told Josef. "The war is going to get here soon. You know what they will do to you if they find out you belong to the Darod clan."

When Josef continued to disagree, Kamaal pointed a finger at Joseph's face and said angrily, "You are not wise."

"Okay, now, stop!" I said to Kamaal, because I could see that Josef was also growing angry and a fight was about to break out. The boys glared at each other but stopped arguing. Later that night, Kamaal came to apologize to me.

"I'm sorry the way I talked to Josef," he said. "I'm sorry you had to see that."

One day Kamaal, Josef, and I went down to the bus station in the center of town to watch who arrived on the buses. When a certain bus pulled into the station, I recognized a woman who stepped off. "Halima, Halima, it's me!" I called and rushed over to her.

We embraced and I started talking, the words rushing nonstop out of my mouth. I was so happy to find a member of my family alive. Soon, though, I noticed that Halima seemed tired and worried, and was somewhat absent as she listened to me and nodded politely. She told me she'd been living in Kismayo for a while now with her two boys and her husband. They were staying with a man Halima did not know. The man knew her husband, and so they were allowed to stay with him until they could find another place.

"I am sorry I can't take you in, too," Halima said. "There's barely enough room for all of us as it is."

"That's okay," I told her. "Kamaal and Josef and I are staying with a very nice man at his café. I will be fine."

Halima glanced sceptically over at Kamaal and Josef. She was very religious and probably suspected that I was having a love affair with one of them. Halima and I couldn't talk long, but she let me know where she was staying and told me to come visit often. After reuniting with Halima, I regained my belief that I would find my family eventually and that we could again have a good life together. Before running across Halima, I'd almost given up hope of every seeing my family members again.

Despite that my living situation was better now, Kamaal, Josef, and I were still cautious and watchful when we moved through the city. There was still a lot of ill-will about Siyaad Barre, which could spill over into violence without warning. Siyaad Barre's nickname was Afweena, which means big mouth. Painted on the walls of the city were several pictures of Barre with a big, open mouth and little kids on the way down his maw. *Siyaad Barre is eating our children*, the posters read. To Barre's opponents, everyone from his clan were big mouths who wanted to eat the future of other people. Like me, Barre belonged to the Marehan clan, a sub-clan of the Darod clan. Everyone from the Marehan clan was particularly vulnerable to having hatred for Barre whiplash back at them. Barre's opponents were constantly broadcasting threats on the foreign radio stations. They hung up posters warning people to hand over Afweena to them. Unfortunately, some Somalian men who were suspected of being in the Darod clan were still getting killed out in the streets for no reason. When Kamaal, Josef, and I walked to the city center together, people stared at us as we walked past, and we were always insecure and uncertain.

Because the level of insecurity was growing daily in Kismayo and elsewhere, Bashi told us that he needed to leave and make sure his wife was okay. He would stay away for a week, and if the war situation grew worse, he would not come back. If the enemy made it to Kismayo and the war continued, then Bashi wanted his whole family to stay with his grandparents on the island. "You're welcome to come along," he told us.

We appreciated the offer, but what about our families? We had to find them, and we wouldn't be able to do that on a remote island. The boys and I agreed to stay in Kismayo for a bit longer and wait for our families. Bashi locked up all the rooms and the restaurant since he wasn't sure when or if he was coming back. He said we were welcome to continue sleeping in the hallway, which was as large as a room. He gave us rice, oil, and canned tuna for food. We were sorry to see Bashi leave, who had been like a guardian angel to us, but were happy we had a place to stay as well as 100 shillings we hadn't spent yet.

Once Bashi left, my daily routine fell into a familiar pattern. Every day, I had three jobs to do. First, I continued to check the bus stations three times a day in the hope I would spot another family member. Sometimes I went alone because I'd noticed no one paid much attention to me when I wasn't with Kamaal and Josef. Secondly, I visited Halima every morning. I was tired of hanging out with men all the time and needed the companionship of women. Also, staying at Bashi's place all day was boring, and walking to Halima's place was a stimulating experience because the neighborhood she lived in was a beautiful area—by the beach on a hill overlooking a harbor and the sea. Lastly, late in the afternoon, I cooked a meal for the boys and myself. Our food rations were scarce so we could only afford to eat once a day. We were already thin, and now we lost even more weight. Still, we tried to remain optimistic and told each other that things would be all right.

Most days I wrote a couple of letters to family members, and then would take the letters to the bus station and ask people what city they were traveling to. I asked these people to take my letters with them. If they could find someone in the other city who knew my last name, they might be able to locate a family member and get one of my letters to them. I knew this was a longshot, but I was desperate and needed to try every possibility.

But as the weeks passed, I heard nothing from family members, nor did I come across anyone else from my family at the bus station. My hope started fading again.

One day, when I visited Halima, she greeted me with good news. "Your mother is alive!" Halima exclaimed.

I was so relieved I didn't know what to say at first. As it turned out, Halima's husband had been asking people if they'd heard anything about my family, and he'd run across a man who said he'd seen my mother in Baardheere. "Can we go to Baardheere together?" I asked her. "We can find her there."

Halima shook her head regretfully. "My husband wants to stay in Kismayo and find a job," she said. "He doesn't think the war will last much longer. Besides, I have the children."

I pleaded with her to come with me to Baardheere and bring the children with her. "No, I can't leave my husband," she said with finality.

Eventually, I had to drop the idea, but I was growing uneasy by how close the war was moving to Kismayo. I didn't want to stay in the city any longer. I grew more and more lonely, even though I was with Kamaal and Josef, and the city was crowded with people from Mogadishu. Occasionally, I recognized someone out in the streets— an elementary school teacher, a classmate from high school. When we saw each other, we would smile slightly but rarely stopped to talk. The war had made everyone suspicious of each other. No one wanted to risk trusting the wrong person.

One day the fighting arrived just outside Kismayo city limits. We heard that Siyaad Barre had fled again, this time to Baardheere with his generals. Many wounded, both civilian and military, continued to flood into the city. Eventually, we could hear the military gunfire, which reminded me of my war experiences back in Mogadishu.

I suggested to Kamaal and Josef once again that we should travel to Kenya. Bashi had given us a lot of information on how to get there. This time, both Kamal and Josef agreed. Now that Kismayo was becoming so dangerous, it felt like the right time to leave. I went over to Halima's place to tell her that I would leave for Kenya the next day. She told me that two of my cousins, Sharmake and Nuur, were alive and still in Mogadishu. I was very grateful for the information, but it was too late now to travel to my cousins in Mogadishu or my mother in Baardheere. Saying goodbye to Halima was difficult. We embraced for a long while and promised we'd see each other again, even though we both knew we couldn't be certain of that. She gave me $200 for the trip. On the way back to Bashi's place to meet up with Kamaal and Josef, a feeling of emptiness overcame me, and I felt despair that I was leaving Halima behind. I have not seen Halima since then, although I heard she survived the war and still lives in the same house in Kismayo.

By the next morning, half of the city had been occupied by the Hawiye clan. People were running around amongst each other, lost and desperate, stepping coldly over the dead and bloated bodies lying openly in the streets. *War turns people into ugly predators*, I thought. We were all trying to survive and couldn't afford to get lost in sentimentality. Kamaal, Josef and I also ignored the dead bodies because we were hurrying down to the beach to find a boat that would take us away from Kismayo. When we arrived at the harbor, we saw there were already people who had spent the entire night at the beach so they would be first in line for a boat that could sail them to Kenya. Kamaal, Josef, and I waited and waited and stared out over the water, but no boats came. People began to fear the boats and ships had been taken over by the Hawiye clan, which meant we were stranded in Kismayo.

While we were waiting, I recognized someone in the crowd: the popular journalist Cuuke. He was a famous and talented newsreader and Siyaad Barre's private journalist. I had seen him on Somalia's only television channel and had heard him often on the radio. His deep commanding voice didn't fit his small, thin body at all. We hurried over to greet him. He was very talkative, and we had a conversation.

"Where are you three going?" he asked. He kept glancing aside nervously, as if he were afraid of being recognized by people. He was alone and not wearing shoes, which seemed strange for someone I thought had so much money, but maybe he'd had to leave in a hurry like the rest of us.

We told him we wanted to try and take a boat to Kenya. I was curious why Cuuke was fleeing, since he was a journalist, and I thought his status would protect him. We had learned in school that if war breaks out in any country, there are five types of people you shouldn't kill: the doctor, the nurse, the priest, the schoolteacher, and the journalist. Besides, Cuuke wasn't a member of the Darod clan.

"Why are you fleeing?" I asked him. "You could write a lot of stories about the war and what's happening."

He shook his head anxiously. "I'm wanted by the Hawiye clan," he said, and it was only then I noticed the fear in his eyes. "I can't trust anyone anymore. People who have worked for Barre's government risk getting killed in very barbaric ways. You can get roasted or cooked alive."

I thought back to my neighbor in Mogadishu, and the boiling pot out in the street, and my neighbor's wife and children begging for his life. I couldn't bear to remember, so I pushed the memory to the back of my mind.

Out on the sea a small white speedboat appeared. The people on the boat shouted that they couldn't make it all the way to the beach, so everyone started darting into the water. Kamaal and Josef charged ahead, and I sprinted after them, the water splashing around me. Twice I fell and inhaled water into my nose and mouth. I rose from the water coughing and spitting but kept moving forward. Suddenly, I couldn't touch the bottom anymore. I was out in the shark-infested Indian Ocean, and I couldn't swim. I floundered, gasping, my lungs burning, but continued to inch my way forward. Finally, Kamaal and Josef grabbed hold of me and helped pull me the last stretch into the boat.

The boat was small, designed for only ten people, but already there were twenty-three of us onboard. Now the boat owner demanded payment from all of us. I was surprised when Cuuke said he had no money. Kamaal, Josef and I had $300, including the $200 that Halima had given me. The boat owner started by demanding $200 from each passenger. Everyone began to complain that it was too much and refused to pay. We argued him down to $100 apiece. But once Kamaal, Josef, and I had paid the boat driver, we had no money left. One boy on the boat gave us $50 so we would at least have a little money to eat once we arrived onshore. Other people on the boat paid Cuuke's fare. The boat owner, satisfied with his money, handed out fishing lines to two of the men onboard who caught us fish to eat. Another young man who worked as a helper on the boat prepared couscous and fish for us. I was nervous that most of the people on the boat were men and that I was one of the only women. I stayed close to Kamaal and Josef, and if anyone asked, we said that I was their cousin. It was abnormal for a woman to sail alone to another country without family or her husband.

We spent the night in a small coastal village, since no one dared to sail at night. There were only four girls in the boat, and we were allowed to sleep on the floor inside an empty café. All were young women in their twenties who came from middle class or upper-class families. One young woman talked about how she was "dead in love" with the man she'd been with on the boat. While most of us constantly talked about trying to find our families, this young woman said she and her boyfriend were hiding from theirs. They'd been hiding since before the war broke out.

"But why?" I asked her. "Why hide from your family?"

"Because my family is rich," the girl told me. "They do not want me to marry a poor man."

The next morning, we started sailing early. At noon, we arrived at a small passage between two cliffs. The sea was rough, and the boat owner said there was a great risk that sharks would attack the boat as we were trying to sail between the cliffs, and then the boat might capsize. We decided to hike over the cliff and meet him on the other side. Unfortunately, hiking over the cliff took several hours, and we needed to make sure we reached the other side before sunset, or the boat would leave without us. It was difficult to walk up the path because it was so steep and rocky with wood and overgrown weeds jutting out of the ground. People quickly became tired and thirsty from the heat and complained to each other about the amount of time it was taking. The men who drove the boat had not been honest with us about how long the hike over the cliff would take. At one point, Cuuke, who was not wearing shoes, stubbed his foot and was in a lot of pain. I saw that his bare feet had several bloody cuts from the sharp rocks, so I gave him one of my sandals to wear. I felt sorry for Cuuke because he was older than the rest of us, which must have made the climbing more difficult. His feet bled quite a bit until one of the girls gave him a drug that was supposed to help stop bleeding.

We grew more worried as the hours passed and we still weren't on the other side. We didn't want to get left stranded on an uninhabited island. We helped each other out as much as possible. The woman who'd said she was "dead in love" with her boyfriend was getting carried on the man's back. The two seemed oblivious to the struggle of the rest of us; they were blinded by love. A couple of times I fell as I was climbing the cliff and Kamaal helped me to my feet. Josef stuck close to Cuuke the whole time and helped him when he needed it. When I gave one of my shoes to Cuuke, a girl approached me and asked, "Are you a rebel? Do you belong to the Communist Youth Party?"

I didn't care to talk to her and stayed as close as I could to Kamaal and Josef.

By the time we reached the other side of the cliff, it was already half dark. The boat was not there. We waited for a while and started to worry that either the boat had capsized and the skipper had been eaten by the sharks, or we had been cheated and the boat man had sailed away without us. Only at sunset did the boat finally appear, bobbing on the water, but by then we were too tired to sail any further. We slept on the beach that night.

Finally, the next afternoon we reached a small town named Kamboni at the Kenyan border. A beautiful 20-year-old boy was sick and vomiting a lot over the side of the boat. Everyone got off the boat and decided whether to take a bus or a car to the nearest Kenyan city. Kamaal, Josef, and I wanted to get to Mombasa even though we had no money to pay anyone. All the money we had we'd given to the boatmen. We only had the $50 someone on the boat had given us for food. Before we headed off to Mombasa, we decided to stay with the sick boy. He was very weak, plagued with severe chills, and continued to vomit even when he was off the boat. I wasn't sure why he was so sick. Some said he had yellow fever while others said malaria.

Two days later, the boy died in Kamboni. Kamaal, Josef, and I were shaken up by his death, yet another reminder of how easily any of us could die. We decided to stay long enough to help bury him. We also called the deceased's family in England as we could not call the family in Somalia. Most of the telephone lines were down in Somalia and disconnected.

The Zoo

The day after we buried the boy, Kamaal, Josef and I took the bus from Kamboni to Mombasa to the Mombasa Zoo, which had become a refugee camp for Somalians. It was a long process before we were allowed inside. All buses and people were stopped one or two miles before they reached the refugee camp. We were herded off the bus while security guards checked us and the bus to make sure we weren't armed or carrying explosives. Then we were allowed to re-enter the bus. We also had to prove we were Somali refugees. The charter bus we were riding carried only refugees, and they had a list with our names, where we came from, and where we were going to. All of this had to be checked and approved at the border before we were allowed into The Zoo.

When we reached the camp, there were several guards at the entrances. Our names were read off one at a time, and when we heard our name, we had to get off the bus and walk into a small office where we were required to fill out paperwork before we gained access to the camp.

It was dark when Kamaal, Josef, and I finally entered The Zoo. Relief flooded over me. Now we were in a place safe from the war and the constant violence and instability. Many refugees hurried over to us as we filed through, eager to know if we'd seen their families, or to get more information about the war in Kismayo.

A guard told me that I needed to turn right and head off with a female guard, and the boys had to turn left and head off with a male guard. I didn't like the idea of separating from Kamaal and Josef, but the camp was divided into three wards: men, women, and families. There was nothing we could do about it.

"We'll come visit you tomorrow," Kamaal promised.

"Okay," I said, dejected. The relief I'd briefly felt changed back to insecurity and fear that I was going to be alone again. The boys and I separated, and I walked along with the other women, feeling empty and abandoned. Kamaal and Josef were not my family, but they were the only ones I knew in the camp, and I felt connected to them.

I grew increasingly uneasy once I was fully inside The Zoo. Before the area had become a refugee camp, it had been a zoo, and all the animals had been moved to make room for refugees. The air was still thick with the pervasive smell of trash, carnivores, animal pee, and unwashed bodies. The toilets were disgusting, with urine puddles on the floors and flies swarming around the holes of human excrement. Every day, new refugees poured into The Zoo, and the space became more and more crowded. The only small advantage I had was that there were many more male refugees than female, so my side of The Zoo was less crowded than the ward for men and the ward for families.

Still, every night people had to compete for a sleeping space, including those of us living in the women's ward. Refugees lay inside, under, and on top of the cages.

The first night I slept in a cage that had once housed rabbits. The rabbity smell still clung to the air, and bugs had overtaken the cage. The next day I had tick bites all over my body from where they'd sucked my blood. Other women complained they had been bitten by snakes.

Because I did not have a residence permit, I wasn't allowed to leave The Zoo. If I left the camp and met a policeman, he would ask for my residence permit, and if he found out that I didn't have one, I could get taken back to the Somalian border. The police knew there were plenty of illegal refugees in Kenya but could be bribed to ignore them. Some people from the camp took a risk by going into the center of Mombasa. Everyone knew that if they did this, they had to be careful and avoid the police if possible.

I had no money now that I'd spent all the money Halima had given me for the boat ride to Kamboni. I also had no clothes other than what I was wearing, and I had no idea of how to survive in Kenya, or what my next step should be. Kamaal and Josef came to visit me the next day as we had agreed, but after that we started seeing less of each other. There were a lot of people in the camp, and we didn't need to depend on each other as much as we once had. I felt more and more isolated from them, and eventually I realized I was truly alone now and could only depend on myself. But what I should do next remained unclear. I grew quiet and felt sad and tired most of the time.

One day I grew bold and decided to risk taking a bus into Mombasa to see if I could find a job. Having a little money would help give me more choices, and I'd prefer to work than sit around The Zoo all day and sleep and sulk. I tagged along with some people who bribed the guards to let us out of The Zoo so we could go into town.

When I reached town and was walking off on my own, I recognized a couple of men who also lived in The Zoo. They sat drinking tea and chewing khat at an outdoor cafe. Soon they recognized me as well.

"Hello, little lady, where are you going?" one of them called out.

I walked over and told them I was looking for a job. They both laughed outright.

"You'll never find a job in Kenya," the man said. "You're a refugee. There's high unemployment anyway. You don't have a residence permit, and you don't speak Swahili."

I grew annoyed with their pessimism. "It's true I don't speak Swahili," I said. "I guess I will have to make do with the English I learned in high school." I said goodbye, turned on my heel, and walked away before the men could say anything more.

As I walked toward the city center, I grew fascinated by the city and how different it looked from Mogadishu. The buildings were in a completely different style, tall and new with many glass windows. There were also several English-style villas with small rows of houses and well-kept gardens in front. Many of the houses were painted red and yellow, unlike the houses in Mogadishu, which were usually white and the buildings in the city center quite old. The cars drove by very quickly and had the steering wheel on the righthand side. Finally, I stepped inside a big shop that sold clothes for both men and women, as well as perfume, shampoo, and makeup. I glanced around for someone who looked like an employee.

A young saleswoman approached me. "Can I help you?" she asked.

I gathered up my nerve. "I'm looking for a job," I said. "Do you need a new employee?"

The saleswoman looked quietly at me. "Are you from Somalia?" she asked.

"Yes," I said, my heart already sinking.

"I'm sorry, we're not allowed to hire anyone from abroad. I doubt you can get a job anywhere in town. You need to watch out for the police. You should probably go back to your camp."

Disheartened, I thanked the young woman and headed back toward the bus stop. I just missed a bus and had to wait for the next one. On the other side of the street, I saw a small restaurant and decided to try my luck there. At least it wouldn't hurt to ask about a job.

But as I was crossing the street, I heard someone yell in a stern voice, "Hello there, you!"

When I turned, I saw two police officers smiling at me from a side street that was well-hidden from the main street. "Me?" I asked nervously.

They motioned for me to come to them. I didn't know how to refuse, so I obeyed. One of the officers was an older man, about forty or fifty, with a beard and big red eyes. The other policeman was young, overweight, and spoke loudly. "Can I see your residence permit?" the younger one said with a wicked smile.

I could tell he enjoyed acting tough and bothering me. I turned to the older man, but he just stared at me with an eerie gaze and was silent. Both men scared me, and I didn't know how to handle a situation with the Kenyan police. I'd heard that the Kenyan police were corrupt and not only because they accepted direct bribery.

A sharp chill ran down my spine, but I tried not to show any fear. "I live at The Zoo," I said, trying to keep the quaver from my voice. "I'm waiting for the next bus."

The officer shook his head and glanced over at his older partner, then back at me. "You are not allowed outside the refugee area without a residence permit," he said angrily. "We will have to arrest you for this."

Now I couldn't even pretend not to feel frightened and trapped. "What have I done?" I asked, and when they ignored me and whispered to each other, I asked again, "What have I done?"

"You are in Kenya without permission," the young officer said.

"But there are thousands of Somalian refugees in Mombasa," I reminded them. "I'm just one of them. We'll all go back to Somalia as soon as the war is over."

But they only laughed and indicated I needed to follow them. I glanced around the street but there were no Somalians around to see me go off with the officers. The fear of getting raped or killed crept over me. I started to cry and didn't know what to say to convince them to let me go. The officers ignored my tears as we walked along.

When we'd veered off onto a side street, they stopped walking and turned to me. "Would you like to go back to The Zoo instead of prison?" they asked.

I nodded even though I was afraid to hear what they had in mind.

"If you can pay us with money or gold, we'll let you go," the officer said.

I was so tired of having to pay men to help me out of bad situations, but I knew I had no choice. I had twenty Kenyan shillings that two girls at The Zoo had given me, that I had saved to buy a ticket to Nairobi. I handed the money over to them, but they still weren't satisfied, since it only added up to the equivalent of about two or three dollars. "This is not enough," the young officer said. "It's way too little. We can't allow you to go for just this."

I shook my head helplessly. Then I remembered I had an old watch that had been given to me by one of my uncles when he was in the United States. "I have this expensive watch," I said and handed it over to him, even though it was quite cheap.

The two officers examined the watch and turned it over in their hands. "You can keep the watch and give the twenty shillings back," I said.

The officers sneered at me but seemed happy with the watch. They walked off with both the watch and the twenty shillings.

I was both relieved and disgusted. The officers were greedy and petty and squeezing whatever money they could out of the refugees, who had very little as it was. Because I had no country to call home, they felt empowered to take advantage of me and treat me like I was worthless. My disgust quickly turned to anger. I ran back to the bus stop and barely caught the next bus. The driver asked for money for the ticket. I didn't know what to say to him. There were other Somalians in the bus, and I just stood there, defeated, and said nothing. Eventually, a middle-aged Somalian man stood up and paid for my ticket. "Do you speak English?" he asked. He assumed I wasn't answering because I didn't understand what was being said.

I sat next to the man and told him what the police officers had done. He shook his head and told me, "If you had been together with others, that would not have happened."

I didn't dare leave The Zoo after that. I just lay on the ground in an abandoned cheetah cage and cried most of the day. A few of the other women came to check on me and see how I was doing. They brought me tea and told me to pull myself together. We were all in the same predicament, they said. I knew that what the police officers had done to me had occurred also to many others, and no Somalian could find a job in Kenya, but I still felt humiliated and personally attacked. Everything bad that had happened to me was a result of being a foreigner and a refugee. I had no control over that. I had always wanted to travel and experience the world, but now that I was on foreign soil, I felt alien and unwelcome and began to seriously miss my homeland.

One of the girls from the camp approached me and told me I should spend more time with the other girls and try to have fun. "You sleep all day like a lion puppy," she said.

I shrugged. "I used all my energy escaping from Mogadishu," I told her. "Now I just need to relax."

Another day an elderly woman sat down beside me and didn't say a word. At first, I was uncomfortable with her silence. But then she started to cry and told me that her daughter had died last week. I consoled her and told her I didn't know if my own family was alive or dead.

"I bought a dress and scarf for my daughter as a gift," the old woman said. "I was going to give it to her when we met." She looked over at me and sighed. "My daughter is not coming," the old woman said. "You can have the dress and scarf."

I didn't know what to say other than "thank you." I'd never received such a sad and heartfelt gift before.

I started thinking about going to Nairobi. I'd heard rumors that Somalis in Nairobi were staying in hotels and not refugee camps, and that they were free to walk the city. Here in The Zoo, there were guards all around, and we had little freedom. The Zoo was very much like a prison. The setting and atmosphere were eerie, with men separated from women, and guards monitoring all our moves. We weren't allowed to go into the city to work or to do anything unless we bribed the guards first. The guards were also violent at times. They beat a couple of young Somali men who tried to run away from The Zoo. I'd been told there were Kenyan guards who'd raped a Somali woman, and when she complained, the Kenyan took her away from the camp. No one knew where she was taken or what had happened to her. Some people believed she'd been killed, and her body thrown out in the woods. I didn't know what to believe but knew that I had to be careful.

One day when Kamaal and Josef came over to visit me, I asked them if they wanted to go with me to Nairobi. Unfortunately, they said they wanted to stay in Mombasa and wait for their family. I didn't know if I could handle the trip to Nairobi all by myself. Kamaal and Josef were lucky because they had quickly found their big brother and his wife and were told that their mother and father were in Kismayo. They could not see a future in Kenya and wanted to return to Somalia as soon as possible.

I spent a few more weeks in The Zoo, trying to figure out my next move. There was nothing to do while I waited. I continued to sleep a lot and eat with a few of the girls and occasionally talk with them. I had no money and no way to buy food for myself at the store in The Zoo or from the many food vendors who passed through during the day. A few of the other girls shared their food with me so I wouldn't go hungry. Otherwise, camp life was very isolating.

Finally, I decided to head off to Nairobi on my own. I was tired of the crowds and the boredom of refugee life. I felt stuck in The Zoo and needed to try and improve my life. I borrowed $200 Kenyan shillings from a girl whose sister lived in London and had sent her $500. With that money, I could buy a bus ticket.

It was hard to say goodbye to the boys, especially to Kamaal. We had stayed together the whole way and had gotten to know each other well. Before I left for Nairobi, Kamaal and Josef came over to my side of the camp for a final visit. We sat outside for several hours, and I made tea for them. Eventually, we started to reminisce about the hardships we'd faced together.

"Remember when you lied to the driver and told him I was your husband and Josef was your brother-in-law?" Kamaal asked.

We all laughed at the memory. It felt freeing to laugh about something that had been so serious at the time. "You were a good liar," Josef said.

We all agreed to that too. Josef had been good at remaining quiet and invisible and to not appear threatening. Kamaal's gift had been to reason with people and pose relevant questions. And my role had been to negotiate with drivers and other men who wouldn't listen to a guy, and to lie when necessary. Each of us, I thought, had played a part in helping all three of us survive.

Kamaal suggested we walk down to the stretch of beach that was accessible from The Zoo. As we walked, I made one last attempt to convince them to come with me to Nairobi. "Come on," I said impatiently. "What is there to do here every day?"

Kamaal and Josef were silent for a moment, and they looked at each other before they answered. "We can't, Qaali," Kamaal said. "We want to stay a few more weeks and see if any more of our family shows up."

I was sad and disappointed to hear this, even though I couldn't fault them for holding onto the hope that they would reconnect with their family. I sighed and said, "This is the last time we are together."

Then I started to cry. Kamaal embraced me and said, "You must not cry." Josef stepped over to us and we stood together in a group hug for a couple of minutes. "We will find you in Nairobi," Kamaal said. "We will find you no matter where you are in the world."

I nodded but knew there was no way to guarantee that. He'd promised his sisters he would find them, too, and so far, he had not. "You do not cry," Kamaal said to me.

Eventually, we sat down on the beach together and watched the sun go down. Josef started to cry a little and wipe at his eyes. We'd been through such an ordeal while on the run together and it was hard not to get emotional. Finally, when it was almost dark, we walked back quietly to The Zoo. "Goodbye," I said again and waved my hand at Kamaal and Josef.

They smiled and waved back. "We will see each other again," Kamaal promised.

Then I watched as the boys turned and walked back to their side of the camp.

I never saw Kamaal and Josef again. A few years later, when I was in Holland, I ran into a woman who knew Kamaal and Josef. She told me that Kamaal was living somewhere in Holland and that Josef was now living in Dubai. Whether the boys ever found their mother or sisters, I don't know.

I planned on taking a night bus to Nairobi. I knew what I was about to do was illegal, since I didn't have a residence permit, and that if the police found out they could put me in jail or send me back to the Somali border. But I was willing to take that risk to get to Nairobi. I asked two girls who were good at bribing the guards if they could help me get out of The Zoo. The girls handed the guards a little money and we walked right through the gate. The girls told me they often went out on weekends to a local bar and disco, and they'd come to know the guards well.

As I sat in the bus and waited for it to leave, I glanced around at the other passengers and saw I was the only Somalian onboard. I could clearly see that I was different: my clothes, my hair, my face. Somalis don't look like Kenyans. Somalis are tall, thin, and fair skin, with long faces and long hair. I was sure the people on the bus could tell I wasn't Kenyan.

I fell asleep while waiting for the bus to depart and was awakened by a policeman. I sat up straight in my seat; I was afraid he was going to demand money. "Could I see your residence permit?" he asked.

The police officer was an older man with a kind face and calm voice, but my heart still

started pounding in my chest. *Stay calm*, I told myself. I pulled out my ID card that stated I was a Somalian refugee and handed it to the police officer.

He squinted at the card and then looked back at me. "Why are you going to Nairobi?" he asked.

"To visit family."

"What's their address?"

Now all my fear had returned, and I was worried about getting arrested. "I don't remember," I said feebly.

The police officer shook his head. "All these Somalian refugees want to go to Nairobi," he said under his breath. Then he handed back my ID card and stepped off the bus.

I was relieved the police officer had left and hadn't taken me into custody. When I glanced around the bus, I saw most of the passengers staring at me, some harshly and some with pity.

Once the bus pulled out of the station, I was excited to leave the refugee camp behind and start a new journey. During the trip to Nairobi, unfortunately, I had no food. I had spent all the money my friend had given me on the bus ticket. A couple of elderly ladies in a nearby seat offered me some food, but I declined the offer and said I wasn't hungry. I was hungry, but it would be too embarrassing to admit that I had no food for myself.

Hotel Hilton

I arrived in Nairobi early in the morning of the next day. A few passengers left the bus, but many remained in their seats. I was confused until one of the elderly women in the seat across from me explained it was best to stay on the bus until it was light and there were more people out in the street. A lot of robberies took place in the cover of darkness. If you left the bus when it was dark, especially if you were traveling alone, you risked getting assaulted.

I nodded and stayed where I was.

At seven o'clock, when light was breaking outside, the remaining passengers began to step off the bus. I also walked out into the street. I was first struck by how cold the air was. I'd never experienced the cold before, and I had no jacket. I glanced up and down the street, unsure which direction to go. I had no money, no clean or warm clothes, and I was alone in an unfamiliar city. I reminded myself not to feel overwhelmed or scared.

Finally, I asked the elderly woman from the bus if she knew where I could find some Somalians. The woman smiled at me and said, "I know there's a Somalian grocer in my neighborhood. I live about a mile away."

I had no choice but to believe her and try to get to that grocer. My heart surged at the thought of connecting with some Somalians who might be able to help me or might know something about my family members. But it was difficult to do much when I had no money. I didn't know how to explain this to the elderly woman.

The elderly woman fetched a big bag from the bus and then asked, "Do you want to come with me?"

Again, I had no choice. I was glad to have someone to show me how to get to the grocer. "Can I help you carry your things?" I asked.

"Thank you," she said and smiled again.

I grabbed one side of the big and heavy bag, and we began to walk together through unpaved streets that were impoverished and largely deserted. A few people were in the process of opening their stores. Gradually, the walking became harder and harder, and soon it felt as if we had walked several miles. I was hungry and tired and simply didn't have the strength to walk for long while also carrying such heavy weight. "Could we take a little break?" I asked the elderly woman, my voice thin and strained.

"We're very close," the woman said. "Not much further now." She looked at me with concern and understanding. "You're hungry, aren't you?" she asked.

I was too weak to deny the truth any longer or let pride stand in my way. I nodded and the old woman stopped, and we set down the heavy bag. She opened it and pulled a piece of flatbread out and handed the bread to me. This was Kenyan bread, which didn't taste at all like Somalian bread. It didn't have much taste at all and was larger than bread I was used to eating, but I took a few grateful bites. Eventually, we picked up the bag again and started walking again. Soon we stopped in front of a small shop with blue walls, a green door, and high stairs leading inside.

"Here is the store," the old woman said.

I set down my end of her bag and thanked her many times. The old woman wished me well and then continued onward with the heavy bag.

Once the elderly woman had moved on, I went into the grocery store. Inside, a Somalian lady was sitting on a chair behind the counter, unpacking cigarettes and stacking them on the shelves. I stood awkwardly for a moment and waited for the woman to notice I was there.

"Hello," I said finally.

The woman in the chair pretended she hadn't heard me. She didn't even turn around to glance my way. Her posture was stiff and upright. Instantly, I sensed I wasn't welcome.

"I was wondering if you know where the Somalians meet," I said.

She stood up slowly from her chair. "They are soon everywhere," she muttered under her breath. She spoke weak Somali, and I had to concentrate hard to understand what she was saying. She looked at me as though she was irritated, as if I were a beggar.

I pressed ahead. "I have family in Nairobi," I told her. "I need help to find them."

The irritated woman turned to someone sitting behind the door and spoke Swahili at them. I didn't understand what she said. Then the woman turned back angrily at me. "I don't work for Somalian refugees, but they come here all the time and ask for my help anyway," she said.

I felt my face turn hot from embarrassment and shame. "I am sorry I disturbed you," I said, my voice breaking. I hurried out of the shop in tears.

For a few minutes, I walked aimlessly around the immigrant neighborhood, crying and lonely. A few people

opening their shops looked at me with pity as I walked past. I
was hoping I would run across some Somalians, but I didn't see
any, so eventually I returned to the area of the grocery store. The
elderly woman whose bag I'd helped carry had directed me to
the grocery store, so my only hope now was to stay close to the
store and see if any Somalian eventually showed up. I sat right
beside the grocery store's staircase and waited.

After a few hours, three men, none who seemed over
thirty, drove up in a smart new Mitsubishi. They were
dressed in clean clothes and seemed happy and carefree.
When they climbed out of the car, I hurried over to them.

"Sorry, may I ask you something?" I asked.

The three men all smiled at once and seemed friendly.
"Yes, of course," one of the men said. He spoke with the
same accent as the woman in the grocery store who had
been rude to me.

"Do you know the Islii neighborhood?"

The man said he did. When I asked, shyly, if they
could maybe give me a ride there, all three of the men said
that wouldn't be a problem, although Islii was rather far
from where we were now.

"Are you alone?" the man asked.

"Yes," I said.

The man smiled again and invited me into the grocery
store run by the angry woman. "No, that's okay," I said. I
didn't want to interact with her again. "I can stay outside."

"Don't be afraid!" the man said. He told me I should
have breakfast and a bath, and afterwards they could drive
me to wherever I needed to go. "Who do you know in
Nairobi?" he asked.

That was a difficult question to answer because I
didn't know anyone. "I'm just looking for someone from

my clan," I said. "They might be able to help me find my family, or maybe someone knows if anyone in my family is in Nairobi."

The men persuaded me to come into the grocery store with them. When we entered the store, the woman turned to look at us, then recognized me. She frowned and still looked angry. I didn't dare say a word to her. As it turned out, one of the three men was married to the angry woman. "Calm down," he said to his wife. "Everything will be okay."

When the angry woman started to protest, he added, "I have a guest with me. Be quiet." Then the three men and I passed through the store and out the back door.

As it turned out, there was a house in back where the angry woman lived with her husband and their three children. The house was very well-kept with a lot of new furniture. There was also a maid who was young, calm, and friendly. She was washing plates and glasses when the men told her to make me something to eat. I was seated at a small table in the kitchen and served ugali (cornmeal) with meat sauce and vegetables and tea with sugar and milk. The maid continued to work nearby while I ate, and the men sat off in another room. I couldn't eat that much because I was very shy and tired.

When I was finished, the maid showed me to the bathroom. First, she spoke to me in Swahili, but when I said I couldn't speak Swahili, we spoke a little English together. The bathroom was luxurious with a full bathtub, clean towels, and shampoo. The maid left me alone while I filled the tub with water and stepped in. It felt strange to bathe in the home of people I didn't know. I picked up a bar of old-fashioned brown bath soap that smelled like honey and started to scrub my arms and legs. This was so much better than bathing at The Zoo. It was my first proper bath since my mother and me were still living in Mogadishu. At some point, I lay my head back against the tub and just relaxed in the soothing water, breathing in the lovely scent of the soap.

I lost track of time. The maid knocked lightly on the door. "Hello, are you okay?" she asked through the door.

I sat upright in the tub. "Yes, yes, I'm coming now!" I called. Somehow, I'd been in the bathtub for an hour. Hurriedly, I dried myself and stepped into my clothes. When I came out of the bathroom, I felt awkward about spending so much time in the bathroom and smiled sheepishly at the maid.

I returned to the living room where the men were sitting, talking business, and drinking tea and Coca Cola. I told them I was ready to go and was pleased to learn that the men knew many people from my clan. We drove away in the new Mitsubishi to an area where there were only Somalians. Now I felt a little like I was at home again. We stopped at a hotel owned by Somalians. When we asked if there was anyone from the Darod clan at the hotel, we were told there were several. This made sense since people from the Darod clan were the ones who'd fled Somalia while people from other clans largely stayed behind, hoping for a new government.

I said I was looking for my family and gave my family name. An old man overheard and approached me. "I know that name," the man said. "I might know your family."

He asked if I had a relative named Hassan. "I have an uncle named Hassan," I said.

"I saw Hassan just the other day," the old man said.

My heart began to beat faster at the prospect of finally getting reunited with a family member. "Are you sure you saw my uncle?" I asked.

The old man nodded quietly. "We talked here at the hotel," he said. "Maybe he will come here tomorrow. A lot of men meet here to talk."

I almost didn't dare believe him. "I can't wait for tomorrow," I insisted. "I have to find him now."

"The hotel he is living at isn't that far away," the old man said. "Hotel Hilton." He glanced over at the three men who had given me a ride. "Maybe your friends can help you find the hotel."

I thanked the old man, and the three men drove me to the Hilton Hotel. I couldn't believe that after months of misery, hardship, and one frustration after another, I was about to meet up with a member of my family. I'd started to fear I would never find anyone from my family again and was alone in the world. When I thanked the men again for their help, they said it was only normal to help one another. "If you need help anytime in the future, we'll be available," they told me.

I spotted Uncle Hassan sitting in a chair in the hotel lobby. When I started over to him, he spotted me and smiled broadly. "Oh, you're alive, dear," he said as he stood up to greet me. "I'm so happy to see you."

My whole body shook as he hugged me. I couldn't stop crying. Relief at seeing a family member overwhelmed me to the point that I could barely speak. The three men who had driven me to the hotel stood behind me and quietly watched my reunion with my uncle. When I explained how the men had helped me, Uncle Hassan thanked them. "Let me give you a little money for your trouble," he said.

But the three men refused the money. "We were happy to help," one of them said.

Once the three men had said goodbye and left the hotel, I received more news from my uncle. He said my mother would be coming to Nairobi in a week. "She'd given up hope that she'd ever see you alive," my uncle told me.

At first, I was surprised and happy to hear this, but after the initial excitement wore off, I wasn't sure if I wanted to see her. Whatever the circumstances, she'd left me behind in the escape from Mogadishu, and had manipulated me to stay with her at the airport despite the dangers of the escalating civil war. If I hadn't listened to her, I would have escaped Mogadishu much earlier and could have avoided the weeks of suffering I'd just survived. I was still angry about that. Part of me wanted to be free of my mother. I didn't feel I could trust her again; she'd nearly cost me my life.

Uncle Hassan gave me $100 so I could go shopping and get my hair done before meeting up with my mother. Also, he suggested that I stay with some girls I knew from Somalia. They had an apartment together and a maid, even though none of them had a job or were so busy that they couldn't cook and clean themselves. Their families sent them money from abroad even though rent and food were not very expensive in Kenya. The girls welcomed me into the apartment, and I got a bed in a corner of the living room. The next day we went shopping on the main street of Nairobi. I bought a jacket and a pair of sneakers. Later, we all had our hair done by a nice hairdresser. Now I had smooth, dark blonde hair instead of long, black, curly hair. I felt like a new person, a young woman in a special dream.

My mother came to Kenya one week later. We met in a small apartment where she would live with a friend. I had a difficult time hugging her because I got flashbacks to our escape from Mogadishu when she left me behind and rode away with the other people in the car. *War makes people an ugly predator,* I reminded myself, but I still couldn't forget how she hadn't fought harder to stay with me. My mother also seemed awkward and nervous, and I sensed she was struggling with a bad conscience. We felt estranged from one another, our previous battles and problems holding us at a distance. Because of this, we didn't talk a lot and my visit with her was brief, not at all like the kind of reunion you would expect between a mother and a daughter who'd been torn apart by war. She had been in town for several days before we saw each other, she said. She'd fled to Nairobi with her big brother when the war came to Baardheere.

"Have you heard anything about Diina?" I asked. "About Wali or Rush?"

My mother shook her head. "I have not heard," she said.

After a short while, I told my mother I needed to go. I'd reached a point where I felt I could manage without her. I was glad to see that she was okay, but I was ready to move on, away from her.

But fate bound me to my mother longer than I'd anticipated. A couple of months after I'd been reunited with her, Uncle Hassan was granted political asylum in Kenya because he'd been a general for Barre's army. Uncle Hassan and I, along with my mother, her brothers and their families, were moved to a closed-off area in Nairobi with clay huts. Later, the Kenyan government decided this place was too expensive for an asylum area, so we were sent far outside the city to live in a giant refugee camp where there were only blankets to provide shelter. There were no roofs or overhangs to protect us from bad weather. Unpleasant memories of life at The Zoo returned to me, and I found living with my mother again difficult. Soon we all grew tired of the overcrowding and the sparse living conditions, and we left the camp and moved around the city, living with various Somali friends and acquaintances. Despite the difficulty of this time, everyone helped everyone else with money and food as much as possible. I returned to living with girlfriends whose company I enjoyed, and my mother lived with women that she knew. Quietly, my mother and I moved ahead with living separate lives.

Out of Africa

When I'd been living in Kenya with friends for a few years, the Kenyan news announced one day that all Somalian refugees would be sent back to Somalia. The country was still one big mess. The Americans had come to try and help restore stability, but there was no peace. The war continued and many people were killed. When I walked past newsstands in the middle of Nairobi, often I saw many newspaper headlines of Somalian women and children dying of hunger. I not only didn't want to move back to Somalia, but I wanted to leave Africa completely. I knew a lot of Somalians who had travelled to the West seeking asylum, and I wanted to live in a peaceful country where I could get an education.

One day my mother talked to a man who smuggled people into Europe. Of course, he asked for a huge amount of money to provide this service. I was never clear about the amount, but I think she paid a lot of money. My mother and I didn't have that kind of money. But my mother was determined to come up with enough money for a ticket. She wanted to remain in Africa but wanted to keep me away from the war and give me the opportunity to escape to a European country and get a fresh start. Every day we heard new death tallies from Somalia. Thousands of human lives were lost in the clans' battles against each other and during the fights against the American soldiers. There was no future in Somalia, and both my mother and I knew it. My mother scraped money together for a ticket by borrowing money from family and acquaintances and by selling all her gold jewelry. Eventually, my mother managed to raise enough money for one person to accompany the smuggler to Europe, although we didn't know what country in Europe.

My mother and I met the smuggler at an out of the way spot in the Nairobi airport. I didn't bring any luggage with me other than a handbag which contained a couple of changes of clothing. He was a small, thin man with grey hair. I think he was Kenyan, but he didn't say anything about himself. My mother said hello and introduced me to him. He didn't answer back. He was wearing sunglasses and didn't seem to want to look in our direction. He was reserved and I could tell he was also nervous. My mother glanced around us to make sure there was no police or security guard around, and then handed the man a brown letter envelope that contained the money. Quickly, the man stuffed the envelope into his bag. Neither of us completely trusted this man, but we had no other options and we had to take the chance. For all we knew, he could be a thief who made up an elaborate story about smuggling to steal the money, or maybe he was sick in the head and intended to harm me once we were alone.

Finally, he gave me instructions about what I should do during the trip. "Don't say anything," he told me. "Let me take care of everything. If you speak, they could figure out you're a refugee."

I followed him to the ticket counter and stood off to the side while he bought my ticket. I didn't say a word while the man presented our passports and spoke to the ticket agents. They asked him several questions, which he answered in a neutral voice. "She's my wife," I heard him answer to one question.

After a couple of minutes, the man had my ticket in hand, and we returned to my mother so I could say goodbye. We both cried and hugged each other because we knew, deep down, that it would be a long time before we saw each other again. Even though I was frightened to fly with a stranger to a new country where I didn't know the language, I also knew I needed to leave my Somalian life behind. There was no other good option.

My mother waited at the airport until the plane took off. When the man and I entered the plane, he sat in a seat two rows in front of me. This was to ensure his own safety in case I was caught leaving the country illegally. He could pretend he didn't know me if I were led off the plane.

Because the man was sitting two rows in front of me, we didn't speak to each other during the entire flight. This was also done to give the appearance that we weren't traveling together. I felt very alone and was worried about how this would end. I had never flown before so was very scared, but I was even more scared of what my future would be like. What if I was discovered as a Somali refugee and was sent back to Somalia? How would I survive? And how difficult would it be to survive once I ended up in a new country and had to start all over again? I had a hard time understanding what the stewards said but didn't dare ask them any questions because the man had warned me against it. The more questions I asked, the more attention I would draw to myself.

After several hours, we landed in an airport. I didn't know if this was our final destination or whether we would change planes. Everyone filed out of the plane. The man remained seated until the plane was mostly empty, and then he came to me. "We get off here," he said.

Once we'd walked off the plane, the man said, "If the police ask you who you are, tell them you are my wife."

We waited for a few minutes in the line at Customs. My anxiety mounted as we got closer to the security checkpoint. When it was our turn at the passport check, I held my breath as the man showed two passports to the uniformed man behind the glass pane. The uniformed man looked at our passports and handed them back without comment. The man and I passed through the checkpoint gate. I was surprised and relieved that my entry into this new country had been so easy.

We went outside and the man hailed a taxi. I was not allowed to see the passports, and he didn't talk to me at all. I thought it was strange that he was still pretending not to know me even though we'd passed through Customs, and we would be sharing a taxi together. A cab pulled up, and the man and I climbed inside. The cab drove us away from the airport. I noticed it was a grey, cold morning and we were passing a lot of tall, strange-looking red houses. The houses and the streets looked nothing at all like the posters from Paris and New York that I'd seen lining the walls of the cafes in Mogadishu.

The cab stopped in the middle of the city outside a large building that many people were hurrying into, some carrying bags and luggage. The man paid the taxi driver and we walked into the building, which turned out to be a major train station. Once inside, the man started talking to me for the first time.

"We separate here," he told me. "I'm traveling to another country. Now you will need to find some people from Somalia who live in this country to help you. If you can't find anyone, you should seek asylum."

I realized I didn't even know what country we were in. When I asked the man, he said, "Denmark. We're in the capital city, Copenhagen."

I knew nothing about either Denmark or Copenhagen, although I'd studied a little European history in high school and had to learn the names of the countries and capitals. Although it was June, the weather in Copenhagen felt cold to me, and my discomfort with the temperature only added to my fear that I was alone in a foreign country where I did not speak the language.

"Please," I begged the man. "Don't leave me here alone."

His face remained expressionless. "I'm sorry, but unfortunately, I have to," he said, although he never said why he had to. He handed me one hundred Danish kroner. "Good luck in the future," he said and walked off, soon disappearing into the crowd.

I carried my handbag to an empty bench, sat down, and cried. I was scared and exhausted, and I didn't know how to ask someone where the asylum center was. A lot of white people passed back and forth in front of me, and no one asked why I was sitting alone and crying. For several hours I just sat there confused and frightened while I tried to figure out my next move.

Eventually, I saw a woman who looked Somali. I ran over to her and asked her if she was from Somalia. To my great delight, she said yes. I explained my situation and asked if she knew the place where I had to go to seek asylum.

The woman looked at me impatiently, and I could see she didn't want to talk to me.

She was in a hurry because she was on her way to teach at a language school, so she couldn't go with me and show me the way. "But I can show you the train you need to take to get to the Sandholm Center," she said.

"What does Sandholm mean?" I asked.

"It's the name of the asylum center for refugees," she said.

The woman led me to the train track from which the train to Allerød would leave. It was an old, dirty, and very busy train area. "You'll need to buy a ticket," she told me.

"Is $100 enough?" I asked.

The woman offered to pay my ticket to Allerød and showed me what train to take. Once I arrived at Allerød, I would need to buy a bus ticket to Sandholm. "I don't think it will cost more than DKK100," the woman said.

Once the train pulled into the station, the woman said, "Good luck with the asylum application" and left me to get aboard the train alone.

Again, I had tears in my eyes, even though I had promised myself I wouldn't cry anymore. But I couldn't help myself. Everything felt so strange and overwhelming. I kept repeating the word *Allerød* in my mind because that was the station where I was supposed to get off the train. I started practicing in English what I would say when I arrived at the Sandholm Center: "*Hello, I am a refugee from Somalia. I am 23 years old and alone.*" Every time the train came to another stop, I craned my neck so I could see out the window to read the name of the station. In the end, I became uncertain about how to pronounce Allerød. I asked an elderly lady sitting across from me if she could help me get off at the right stop.

"I'm getting off before Allerød, so I can't help you get off at the right station," the old woman said.

A young girl was sitting nearby who spoke English. "I'm going to that same station," the girl said. "I'll show you where to go."

I calmed down some after speaking to the young woman, although I kept my eyes on her because I didn't want to miss when she stepped off the train. Finally, when the train was slowing down at another stop, the girl stood up and said, "This is Allerød station."

Once we'd stepped off the train together, I asked where she was going and explained that I needed to get to an asylum center called Sandholm. "I was told I need to take a bus there," I said.

"I know what bus you have to take," the girl said. "I'll show you to the bus stop."

As we walked together, I thanked her several times for her help. I thought the girl was probably a college student, since she looked about 20 years old, seemed relaxed, and understood me easily even though my English was poor.

Once I boarded the correct bus, I felt a little less alone because it was filled with people of different nationalities—Africans, Arabs, Eastern Europeans. I was surprised to see that the bus driver was a woman, because I'd never seen a female driver in Somalia. The driver seemed sweet and calm and was probably used to hearing a variety of different languages, since some of the asylum seekers didn't speak Danish or English. I gave the driver DKK100 and asked for a ticket to the Sandholm Asylum Center. Fortunately, the ticket only cost eleven kroner.

When we reached the Sandholm Center, the driver said in English into her microphone:

"This is Sandholm Asylum Center." Several passengers on the bus stood up to get off. I followed a line of four people into the asylum center. I noticed that most of the people ahead of me had a card that they showed to the doorman at the entrance. The people directly ahead of me in line also wanted to seek asylum in Denmark, and their English was even worse than mine.

Finally, when I reached the doorman, he asked me what I was there for. "I would like to apply for asylum," I said.

He picked up a phone and called the police. The man was cold and intimidating and didn't seem interested in me or any of the others seeking asylum. "Stand over there until the police come," he said to me and the others and pointed to a space a few feet away.

I only waited about thirty minutes before the police arrived, a man and a woman, but it felt much longer because I was so nervous. The other four people standing in line waiting along with me also looked nervous. We didn't say a word to each other the whole time.

"Come with us," the police told us, and the four others and I followed them inside.

We were escorted into a room where there were three other people who were also asylum seekers. The two police officers went back out again and locked the door from the outside. I felt agitated and frightened again. The room was cold and dark, even though it was noon on a Friday in June. Each of us got a very small blanket and a camp bed to lie on. I went over to one of the empty beds and sat down. What would happen now that I'd said I wanted to seek asylum? I glanced around the room at the others. Two Arab men were chatting quietly and seemed to know each other, but everyone else was quiet and glum, all of us caught in this temporary prison.

A half an hour later, a couple of guards brought food to us. I was surprised at the quantity—meat, potatoes, salad, and rye bread. We were told that some interpreters would soon come speak to us. Despite that I was very hungry, the food was cold, and I couldn't bring myself to eat much of it. I was still uncomfortably cold due to the lack of heat in the room. Eventually, the guards came back and told us that everyone in the room would be staying here until Monday, since all the police officers and interpreters were not working over the weekend. The refugees reacted differently to the news. The two Arab men whispered back and forth. A couple of people didn't look like they understood what the police were saying. Most of us just stared at the ground and were silent like animals in a cage.

We were in that cold bare room from Friday noon until Monday morning. The room was attached to a bathroom that we all shared, but the bathroom only contained a toilet and no shower or bathtub. Because of the cold, I slept very little during those three nights. I stayed in one corner of the room and crouched down to keep warm. The two other women in the room slept together on a bed and smiled at me often, while the men mostly stayed on the other side of the room. Despite the distance between me and the men, I was scared to sleep with a bunch of strangers in a room that I couldn't escape from. Five of the asylum seekers were men and that made me uncomfortable, since this was the first time I had to sleep in the same room as a man. I was the youngest of the eight of us in the room and the only one from Africa. Three of the men and two of the women were from Eastern Europe, and the other two men were from Afghanistan. The five men talked to each other occasionally and it sounded like they understood each other, even if I couldn't understand them. Mostly, I kept close to the women because this made me feel safer.

Also, I was worried about how my case would be received. What if I was sent back to Somalia? What if I got to stay in Denmark but didn't like it? I asked myself many questions over those three days.

All of us inside the room for the weekend wondered why we were locked up when the rest of the asylum center was filled with people walking around freely. We could see many Somalians moving back and forth in front of the windows. I thought again about how I had answered the doorman when he'd asked me what I was there for. Had I misspoken somehow? Had the doorman and the police officers misunderstood me, and that was why I was in jail? I thought I had come to a free country and didn't think it was necessary to wait in a prison before I was granted asylum. I did not feel good about any of it.

Finally, Monday arrived. After breakfast we were told that we would be interviewed separately. Half an hour later the various interpreters came to the room. My interpreter was a woman of about thirty years old. She told me her name, who she was and what the interview would be about. She tried to convince me she spoke fluent Somali even though I couldn't understand everything she said. It became apparent that this woman was incompetent and not good with languages but was trying to pass as a good interpreter so she could keep her salary. Otherwise, she was strict and cold and didn't seem to care about the people she was supposed to help.

I followed the interpreter and two police officers to an office, and she said that they would like to take a picture of me. "Sit there," she said and pointed to a black chair in the far corner. I sat down and the police took a picture of me. Then the police began their interrogation. One of the officers, a tall white man, did the most talking while the other wrote down in a notebook what we said. At first, the questions were standard: Who was I? Where had I come from? Where was I going? Why had I chosen to come to Denmark? Why was I seeking asylum here, and why hadn't I stayed in my own country?

The last question surprised me because the answer seemed obvious. "I was fleeing the war," I said. "I was afraid of getting killed."

I had to fill out a sheet of questions in Somali because they needed to see if I could write Somali. They were checking to make sure that I really came from Somalia, because there were many Kenyans who lied and said they were Somalians, and in that way tried to get granted asylum. It took me a long time to write down the answers to all the questions asked. The police officers then asked me more questions, and the questions got more difficult, some that I couldn't answer: Who was the man I'd been traveling with? Where were the passports we'd been traveling with? Who owned the passports?

"I don't know his name," I told them.

"You're lying," said the tall white officer who was doing most of the talking.

I insisted that I wasn't lying. I described the man as best I could, but his face had already begun to blur in my mind. It was clear that the officers were interested in tracking down the man who had smuggled me into Denmark because what he'd done was illegal. They were afraid he would help transport more refugees into Europe, and they didn't want that.

Eventually, I broke down and began to cry. I was scared and drained from being questioned and doubted. "I can't answer any more of these questions," I said.

The interrogating police officer reminded me again that I had to tell the truth. They had refugees lying all the time, he told me, and they needed to make sure I wasn't one of the liars. "We'll talk to you again later," the officer said.

I received a blue card with my name, nationality, and photograph. The card said I was not allowed to leave Denmark. A different female police officer entered the room and showed me where I was to stay temporarily. We entered a large hall where about thirty people, both men and women, from many different countries were milling around. The hall had only a few small windows, but I could see that it was raining outside. I could also hear the voices from people who were passing by outside, although I didn't understand anything the voices were saying.

The police officer pointed to a small bed. "That one is yours," she said sweetly. I noticed that the bed had the same number, 12, as the one written on my card. She also informed me about the rules. Breakfast was served at 6:30, lunch at noon, and dinner at 17:00 hours. I should arrive at the dining hall on time and should always remember to bring my blue card along. If I got sick, I should contact the nurse as soon as possible.

I was still overwhelmed from my interrogation and all the questions, but I tried to smile at the officer. "Thank you very much," I said.

She smiled at me and left the hall. I sat down on the edge of my bed and looked dejectedly around the room. Most of the people in the room were staring back at me.

A New Beginning

I lived for several weeks at the Sandholm Center while awaiting response from my asylum case. While life inside the center was safe, it was also oppressive in many ways. I was not allowed to leave the center for a long time, and I had to carry my blue card around and show it to anyone who asked both inside and outside the center. The Sandholm Center was a wasteland located in an isolated area far from the city. A fence around the center gave the impression of a prison, and there was a military shooting range nearby where I often heard the sharp report of guns. A bus ran past the center a few times a day, but people went into town only when they needed to. They were afraid of getting caught by the police and then expelled from the Sandholm Center. All refugees were given grey winter coats to wear when we were going into the city or riding buses or trains. This was like wearing a uniform because the jacket marked us as refugees.

Life in the refugee center was marked by insecurity and confusion, at least in my experience. I didn't make friends at the center because people mostly kept to themselves. There were no activities offered, and the center didn't offer any educational resources that would help refugees adapt to their new environment. I had to sit around all day, just as I had at The Zoo. The experience of living in the Sandholm Center was not so different from The Zoo, other than we were living inside instead of outside, and we had regular meals and a bed, however uncomfortable, to sleep in instead of sleeping on the ground. In short, living at the Sandholm Center was much like living in a detention center. We were waiting to see if we would be granted asylum or deported back to our own countries. Denmark winters are cold, and the constant wind and rain lowered my spirits constantly. To be a refugee is to lose your soul. You lose your identity, your family, your friends, and your country, so there is nothing left to your life but a bleak emptiness.

After living in the Sandholm Center for a few weeks, I was transferred to another asylum center located in a small town called Jyderup. This refugee center was much improved over the Sandholm Center. In the Jyderup center, we no longer had to carry blue cards or wear the ugly grey jackets to signal we were refugees. We were allowed to travel into the city whenever we wanted, and we were given better food and more comfortable beds. In my free time, I walked a lot and rode the train to town. There was communal dining so we could get to know the other refugees, and a shopping trip to town sponsored by the Red Cross.

While living in Jyderup, I received some unexpectedly happy news. A Somalian man who had a residence permit and lived in Jutland, an island off the coast of Denmark, was visiting my neighbor. We sat around a table out in the asylum center's garden and drank coffee while we talked about how many Somalians lived in Jutland. He told us that there weren't many and that they all knew each other.

Most of them were single men. I asked him if there were any nice Somalian guys in town, and he mentioned a man named Wali.

I doubted the Wali my friend knew was my brother Wali, since the name is common in Somalia, but I wanted to contact this man, just in case. "Do you have his phone number?" I asked.

The next day, I called from a telephone booth at the center. When a man answered the phone and said, "Hello?" I could tell immediately that this was my brother's voice. I didn't know whether to laugh or cry. When Wali heard my voice, his voice turned surprised and enthusiastic. "Qaali!" he said. "Where are you?"

Unfortunately, he didn't have any information about other family members. He'd been disconnected from everyone since the fall of Mogadishu, more than a year ago. "We thought you might be dead," I told him, since when you don't hear from someone in wartime for a long while, you start to believe the person is dead.

After talking to Wali for a few minutes, I felt relieved and thankful. When I hung up the phone, I can't remember if I ran or flew to tell the others in the hall that I had found my brother. I also wrote my mother to tell her that Wali was alive.

The next time I talked to Wali on the phone, he told me that he'd heard my old friend Sara had been shot and killed in Mogadishu. Men from the Hawiye clan found out she was from the Darod clan, invaded her home, and killed her and her father. I was shocked to hear the news. Despite the awkwardness that had developed between Sara and me when she and her family became wealthy, I always considered Sara a good friend. There were many nights when I woke up in a sweat from dreams that men were invading my house or chasing me and trying to kill me or holding guns or knives to my throat. To hear that Sara had really died in such a violent way was disturbing.

Wali told me he'd also heard about our father as well as Rush and Diina. All of them were alive but scattered around in different cities in Somalia. Diina had escaped Mogadishu with a friend and was living somewhere in northwest Somalia. Rush was in the Kismayo area now, and my father was on the Kenyan border, still living his nomadic life with camels. My mother was still in Nairobi. Other family members were not so lucky. Wali told me many men from our family died in the war, including one of my uncles and my mother's older brother. This news was just another reminder of how tenuous life was, and that who lived and who died often seemed random.

After nearly a year in Jyderup, I was transferred to yet another asylum center located a few miles from Jyderup. I was annoyed and frustrated that I was being moved again because it meant I would lose contact with my friends in the Jyderup center. There were many refugees coming and going into the centers, and so the population was always in flux. Because administrators wanted to keep families and children in the city centers to provide better access and opportunities for the children, it was common for young singles such as myself to get moved from place to place, wherever they had room.

At this new asylum center, they started to prepare us for life in Denmark. I was told that Denmark is a democracy where everyone has the same opportunities and freedoms. People are allowed to talk about anything they want to, and women are afforded the same rights as men. I was pleased with what I heard because I still had a strong desire to receive a higher education. I planned to learn Danish in a year and then start studying at a university. I'd lost interest in becoming a nurse because, after everything I'd been through, I couldn't bear the thought of more blood and sick people. Now I wanted to study history or sociology.

Finally, after more than a year in Denmark, I received a residence permit. This meant I would no longer live in an asylum center and would go out into the world and take care of myself in Danish society. I would receive money every month from the municipality so I could pay for food and clothes. The government also provided a room in a house I would share with other refugees.

The day I was released from the asylum center was relatively uneventful. I said goodbye to a few people and the Red Cross staff who worked there. It felt strange to be leaving and letting go, but I knew that was the best option moving forward. I'd received a letter telling me what house I'd been placed at for residence along with instructions about how to get there. And yet no one was going to escort me to the new place. I would take a bus on my own from the asylum center to the train station, where I would catch a train to Næstved. From there I would walk over a half a mile to my new place.

I waited alone at the bus stop outside the asylum center with only my small suitcase and handbag. I wish I could say I felt thrilled and confident that I was starting a new journey. But the truth is that I still felt insecure, uncertain, lonely, and wary of what the future might hold. How would I find my way in this new country when I already felt so fragile and burnt out?

Then I thought about Sara and her father, and Moses, and the overweight man in the dress, and Kamaal and Josef's sisters and cousin, and the man we had buried outside the military pilot's villa, and my neighbor who had been killed in front of his family, and the child raped by the soldiers. They had all been killed or had their lives ruined because of the war. I had survived. As the bus pulled to a stop and I stepped inside, I felt the first stirring of possibility. Yes, my future was uncertain, but at least I still had a future—a life! —stretched out before me, awaiting the next chapter.